H²h
How to Help

Anxiety
Depression
How to Help

Gerri Brady

Anxiety and Depression

© 2022 Pavilion Publishing and Media Ltd

The author has asserted her rights in accordance with the Copyright, Designs and Patents Act (1988) to be identified as the author of this work.

Published by:

Pavilion Publishing and Media Ltd
Blue Sky Offices, 25 Cecil Pashley Way
Shoreham by Sea, West Sussex
BN43 5FF

Tel: 01273 434 943
Email: info@pavpub.com
Web: www.pavpub.com

Published 2022

All rights reserved. No part of this publication may be reproduced, stored in a retrieval system, or transmitted in any form or by any means, electronic, mechanical, photocopying, recording or otherwise, without prior permission in writing of the publisher and the copyright owners.

A catalogue record for this book is available from the British Library.

ISBN: 978-1-80388-046-4

Pavilion Publishing and Media is a leading publisher of books, training materials and digital content in mental health, social care and allied fields. Pavilion and its imprints offer must-have knowledge and innovative learning solutions underpinned by sound research and professional values.

Authors: Geraldine Brady
Cover design: Emma Dawe, Pavilion Publishing and Media Ltd
Page layout and typesetting: Tony Pitt, Pavilion Publishing and Media Ltd
Printing: CMP

Contents

Series Preface 1
About the Author 2
Author's Preface 3
How to Use This Book 5

Part 1: Introduction 9
Chapter 1: What are anxiety and depression? 11
Chapter 2: Prevalence and provision 17
Chapter 3: Causes and consequences 21
Chapter 4: Identifying problems 25
Ten key things to know about anxiety and depression 29

Part 2: Contexts and approaches for support 31
Chapter 5: Where to begin 33
Chapter 6: Talking about difficult feelings 39
Chapter 7: Strategies for soothing and self-regulation 43
Chapter 8: Sleeping, eating and physical self-care 49
Chapter 9: Relaxation, enjoyment and emotional self-care 55
Chapter 10: Challenging unhelpful thoughts 61
Chapter 11: Recognising avoidant behaviours 69
Chapter 12: The school culture and environment 73
Chapter 13: In the classroom 79

Part 3: Common anxiety problems in children and young people 83
Chapter 14: Types of anxiety and when to seek help 85
Chapter 15: Generalised anxiety 91
Chapter 16: Social anxiety 101
Chapter 17: Panic and agoraphobia 111
Chapter 18: Specific phobias 121

Part 4: Other forms of anxiety less common in children and young people 131

Chapter 19: Post-Traumatic Stress Disorder (PTSD) 133
Chapter 20: Obsessive-Compulsive Disorder (OCD) 143
Chapter 21: OCD-related disorders 153
Chapter 22: Separation anxiety 159
Chapter 23: School anxiety and refusal... 167

Part 5: Depression 177

Chapter 24: The teenage brain and mood difficulties..................... 179
Chapter 25: Depression and low mood... 185
Chapter 26: Specific strategies for depression 197

Part 6: Conclusion 203

Chapter 27: Summary 205
Chapter 28: A last word to parents and carers 211
Chapter 29: A last word to teachers and schools 213

Index of *How to Help* advice 215
Appendix 217
References...235

Series Preface

Young people in today's society face considerable stresses. The Prince's Trust, which has monitored youth opinion for ten years, found that just under half of young people who use social media now feel more anxious about their future when they compare themselves to others on websites and apps such as Instagram, Twitter and Facebook. A similar proportion agreed that social media makes them feel 'inadequate'. The *Guardian Weekly* noted in early 2019 that more than half of young people think that social media creates 'overwhelming pressure' to succeed.

There are many issues that are likely to affect every pupil at some point during his or her time at school. How these are dealt with can be 'make or break' for some pupils, because of the crucial stages in education that can be affected. The implications are deep and broad because, understandably, the child's experience of education, and his or her success at school, can have a tremendous impact on later life chances.

The *How to Help* series covers a broad and comprehensive range of topics that will have resonance for today's parents, carers and educators. Each title is designed to make a valuable contribution in the breadth of issues that it introduces, and the realistic helping strategies that it puts forward.

Gavin Reid and Jennie Guise
Series Editors

About the Author

Gerri Brady is a Consultant Psychological Practitioner with First Psychology Edinburgh. She works therapeutically with children, young people and adults, and offers consultations for parents and carers. Gerri also provides clinical supervision for Cognitive Behavioural Therapy (CBT) practitioners.

Gerri uses a range of evidence-based therapies in her work, including CBT and related approaches such as mindfulness-based therapy and compassion-focused therapy. She works with clients with a variety of needs, including phobias, social anxiety, trauma, Post-Traumatic Stress Disorder (PTSD), panic disorder, health anxiety, Obsessive-Compulsive Disorder (OCD), Generalised Anxiety Disorder (GAD), stress, depression and mood issues, anger and irritability, low self-esteem, bereavement, insomnia, relationship issues and adjustment issues relating to life transitions.

Gerri has worked as a psychological therapist in mental health services for more than sixteen years, supporting adults, children and young people with mild to severe difficulties. She has practised in a variety of settings, including primary care adult mental health services, counselling services for university staff and students, and private practice. Prior to her current role, she spent three years working as a Senior Cognitive Behavioural Therapist and Theraplay practitioner in a specialist outreach team for children and young people in primary and secondary schools.

Author's Preface

In today's world, with the increasing prevalence of mental health problems in children and young people, the importance of parents and teachers being able to recognise emotional difficulties cannot be underestimated. This is particularly relevant amid the troubling times of the COVID-19 pandemic. Early intervention, prevention and the promotion of mental health awareness are key to managing the problem. When parents, teachers and mental health professionals work together as a team, this can help enormously in achieving positive outcomes for the young person. It reassures them, providing hope and a sense of being supported and in good hands.

An integral part of what I do in my therapeutic work with children and young people day-to-day is to provide comprehensive, clinical, jargon-free psychoeducation regarding the ways in which they can be affected by anxiety and depression. Teaching them about the nature of their mood difficulties and what is happening to them often brings relief and understanding about how they have been feeling, normalising their experiences.

It is also paramount in this context to offer psychoeducation to parents and educators in order to increase their awareness and understanding of the behaviours they are observing in troubled children and young people. Learning about mental health is equally important for both caregivers and teachers. Some years ago, I worked as a senior psychotherapist in an outreach team that provided mental health support to pupils in schools across a large city. We delivered psychoeducation for teachers and support staff, offering them an insight into how anxious and depressed young people can present in the educational setting. It was very well received, and it confirmed our belief that all teachers would benefit from being given this kind of information as part of their training. Fortunately, in recent years, the government has committed to the provision of mental health training for all secondary school educators.

The purpose of this book is to convey an optimistic and encouraging message to parents and teachers regarding the benefits of gaining mental health knowledge and awareness. It is hoped that they will then feel empowered and better informed about what to look out for and how to respond if they sense that a young person could be suffering with emotional difficulties.

The book will begin in Part 1 with an overview of anxiety and depression, including a brief history of approaches to treatment and details of the diagnostic features for each condition. It will also present current government initiatives, research findings and statistics around the prevalence of mental health problems in our children and young people

Part 2 offers strategies and practical guidance for parents and teachers to support children and young people with emotional difficulties. This includes a range of evidence-based coping and self-soothing strategies for managing anxiety and depression, and for improving emotional wellbeing, resilience and day-to-day functioning.

Parts 3-5 contain individual chapters on the various types of anxiety and depression. It is important to note that these conditions can often coexist at the same time. Each chapter presents a real-life anonymised case study, detailing how a particular child or young person was helped to recover. There is *How to Help* guidance for each condition, in addition to information on how parents and teachers should proceed if they feel that onward referral may be necessary. Finally, Part 6 brings the various themes of the book together and offers a last word to readers.

Gerri Brady

How to Use This Book

Topics in this *How to Help* book are organised within four major sections, comprising Parts 2 to 5:

- Contexts and approaches for support
- Common anxiety problems in children and young people
- Other forms of anxiety less common in children and young people
- Depression

Within these sections, each topic is discussed in a separate chapter (although it should be noted that in practice there will frequently be areas of overlap), with advice for parents, carers, teachers and schools. You can read through the sections in order or go straight to what concerns you most. The topics have been chosen to represent the key issues that typically arise when seeking to parent, teach, support and understand children and young people who are experiencing anxiety and depression.

Whenever you see the *How to Help* icon, you can expect to find practical, ready to use suggestions and strategies for helping children and young people to cope with anxiety and depression and to maintain healthy levels of wellbeing and functioning.

We recommend that you read in full the Introduction (Part 1) and the Conclusion (Part 6). The former serves as an entry point to the main chapters, presenting the subject and core principles relating to it along with a list of ten essential things to know. The latter summarises the most important points for readers to take away, and offers final comments for parents, carers, teachers and schools.

To keep up to date with the *How to Help* series, bookmark:
www.pavpub.com/howtohelp

"And the day came when the risk to remain tight in a bud was more painful than the risk it took to blossom."

Anaïs Nin

Part 1: Introduction

Chapter 1: What are anxiety and depression?

A brief history of anxiety and depression

Contemporary medical and psychological researchers and practitioners work together in close collaboration to understand mental health and its links with physical wellbeing. Our attitudes and knowledge regarding the features and causes of anxiety, depression and other conditions have been developed and refined over an extended period of time, and today we have a good understanding of the major mental health difficulties together with clear guidelines, coping strategies and a range of evidence-based therapies. Needless to say, this was not always the case.

> **Key Point**
>
> *Today we have a good understanding of mental health difficulties together with clear guidelines, coping strategies and a range of evidence-based therapies.*

In ancient times, there were two distinct schools of thought with regard to psychological and physical health. Greek philosophers such as Socrates and Plato described themselves as 'doctors of the soul' and the human mind, theorising about spirituality, human emotion and mental illness. Physicians and apothecaries, meanwhile, focused on physical illnesses. Eminent physicians such as Hippocrates argued that medical disorders and illnesses were caused by deficiencies or imbalances in the four main *humours* or fluids in the human body (blood, phlegm, yellow bile and black bile), while Aristotle perceived anxiety and depression as medical disorders. Interestingly, however, even in those ancient days there were glimmers of what is now known as cognitive psychology – a recognition that negative thinking plays a central role in the persistence of anxiety and depression.

Fast forward to the seventeenth century and we find anxiety classified as *panophobia hysterica* and *panophobia phrontis*. *Panophobia hysterica* was a state of panic and associated vapours, an archaic term for hysteria and depression. *Panophobia phrontis* was the fear or worry of the unknown, and a sense of panic and uncertainty resulting in avoidance and *melancholic* states of mind. These categorisations had similarities with our current classification of generalised anxiety, and the recognition of a link between anxiety and the development of comorbid depression.

The scholar Robert Burton (1577-1640) recognised the connection between depression and anxiety, which he defined as *melancholia*. In his book *The Anatomy of Melancholy*, published in 1621, he proposed that *melancholia* encompassed both sorrow (depression) and fear (anxiety). He also integrated this with Hippocrates' model of the four humours in the body which were believed to govern health and wellbeing. Burton recognised the link between the mind and the body. He described how the symptoms of melancholy affected the body, and the ways in which this could relate to physical and mental health. He also explored the causes and potential methods of treating depression and anxiety.

Although these developments took place over four hundred years ago, they have correlations with how we think about physical and mental health today, albeit using alternative theories and models. As time moved through the eighteenth and nineteenth centuries, anxiety and depression were recognised as being closely interrelated. This relationship was classified as *neurasthenia*, characterised by symptoms of both depression and anxiety with emotional exhaustion and physical fatigue as the main symptoms. In the late 1800s, William Cullen used the terms *neurosis* or *nervous disorder* to describe mental health problems such as anxiety and depression which did not have obvious organic causes.[1] Then, in 1895, Sigmund Freud used the term *anxiety neurosis* to describe and encompass anxiety and associated mental health difficulties relating to ego responses and repression.[2]

The twentieth century was a period of rapid progress in our understanding and treatment of mental disorders. In the 1950s, two antidepressant drugs were developed to treat both depression and anxiety. Progressive muscle relaxation exercises were also introduced to address symptoms of anxiety and low mood. In the 1970s, Stanley Rachman developed exposure and response prevention treatment for Obsessive-Compulsive Disorder (OCD) and anxiety.[3] This involved gradually and repeatedly exposing individuals with anxiety to their triggers. The rationale was to reduce avoidance, and to desensitize or mitigate anxious responses to feared situations.

In the 1980s and 1990s, developments in pharmacology, neuroscience and brain imaging allowed scientists to observe that antidepressant medications improved symptoms of both anxiety and depression by supplementing deficits in positive neurotransmitters such as dopamine and serotonin. Sufficient levels of these substances help to improve low mood, and antidepressants were therefore more widely introduced to

---

1 Knoff, W.F. (1970) A history of the concept of neurosis, with a memoir of William Cullen. *The American Journal of Psychiatry*, 127(1), 80–84.
2 Crocq, M.A. (2015) A history of anxiety: from Hippocrates to DSM.
3 Rachman, S. (2015) The evolution of behaviour therapy and cognitive behaviour therapy. *Behaviour Research and Therapy*, 64, 1-8.

reduce symptoms and prevent relapse. Antidepressants are sometimes recommended for young people today if 'talking therapies' alone have not been sufficient to alleviate high and enduring levels of anxiety and depression. However, clinical research continues to explore evidence of possible unhelpful side effects and contraindications, and to establish how advisable and effective these medications are for this age group.

Mental health today

In the twenty-first century, modern sciences such as psychiatry, psychology, pharmacology and neuroscience have joined forces to better understand human emotions and behaviours and to carry out research into the efficacy of various treatments. There is now a more holistic approach to mental health, one that considers the relationship between physical, emotional, social and spiritual wellbeing. It has also been recognised that the health of the mind and the body are inextricably linked.

> **Key Point**
>
> There is now a more holistic approach to mental health that considers the relationship between physical, emotional, social and spiritual wellbeing.

Today, rather than thinking about mental health in terms of disconcerting labels like *hysteria, melancholy* and *neurosis*, conditions such as anxiety and low mood have been demystified. They are now seen as normal, treatable human difficulties. Thankfully, draconian and inhumane treatments such as trepanning (drilling holes in the skull) and the bleeding or purging of *humours*, mystical rituals, the administration of strange potions, ice-water baths, and extreme psychosurgery are things of the past.

Thanks to the rigours of ongoing clinical research and advancements in the medical and psychological sciences, we now know much more about the possible causes of anxiety and depression. We also have clear, accessible diagnostic criteria to help us identify these conditions and recognise how they may present in our children and young people.[4,5] Mental health professionals have diagnostic questionnaires and inventories to enable them to detect symptoms, and to assess individual levels of anxiety and depression. These are then used to measure progress during therapeutic interventions, and to provide helpful information on outcomes.

---

4   World Health Organization (2021) *ICD-11: International Classification of Diseases 11th Revision.* Available at: https://www.who.int/standards/classifications/classification-of-diseases

5   American Psychiatric Association (2013b) *Diagnostic and Statistical Manual of Mental Disorders (DSM-5).* Arlington, VA: Author.

Defining anxiety and depression

Anxiety may be defined as:

> "An emotion characterized by feelings of tension, worried thoughts and physical changes. People with anxiety disorders usually have recurring intrusive thoughts or concerns. They may avoid certain situations out of worry. They may also have physical symptoms such as sweating, trembling, dizziness or a rapid heartbeat."[6]

Depression may be defined as:

> "More than just sadness. People with depression may experience a lack of interest and pleasure in daily activities, significant weight loss or gain, insomnia or excessive sleeping, lack of energy, inability to concentrate, feelings of worthlessness or excessive guilt and recurrent thoughts of death or suicide."[7]

The National Institute for Health and Care Excellence (NICE), which advises the National Health Service (NHS) on best practice, recommends Cognitive Behavioural Therapy (CBT) for the management of mild to moderate mental health problems such as depression and anxiety.[8,9] While there is a wealth of evidence to support this, the NHS also recommends other therapeutic interventions according to individual presentations and ongoing clinical research. In 2007, the Department of Health invested in the training of therapists and the provision of CBT within the NHS for adults. In 2011, it went on to outline the development of a similar service for children and young people.[10] This programme brought together Child and Adolescent Mental Health Services providers from both the statutory and voluntary sectors, with the aim of improving access to effective mental health services and support.

To some extent, anxiety and low mood can be natural and understandable responses in children and young people to the various stages of their emotional development and the events in their lives. However, it is crucial

---

6 American Psychological Association (2021) *Anxiety*. Available at: https://www.apa.org/topics/anxiety

7 American Psychological Association (2021) *Depression*. Available at: https://www.apa.org/topics/anxiety

8 National Institute for Health and Care Excellence (2011) *Common mental health problems: identification and pathways to care: Clinical guideline [CG123]* Available at: https://www.nice.org.uk/guidance/CG123/chapter/1-Guidance#steps-2-and-3-treatment-and-referral-for-treatment

9 Royal College of Psychiatrists (2021) *Cognitive Behavioural Therapy (CBT): for Parents and young people*. Available at: https://www.rcpsych.ac.uk/mental-health/parents-and-young-people/young-people/cognitive-behavioural-therapy-(cbt)-for-parents-and-young-people

10 https://assets.publishing.service.gov.uk/government/uploads/system/uploads/attachment_data/file/213765/dh_123985.pdf

to be vigilant and to recognise if low mood or anxiety are pervasive and adversely affecting the young person's wellbeing and ability to function. Research shows that early detection and intervention can protect children and young people from having difficulties in later life.[11]

Both anxiety and depression are highly treatable. It is important and reassuring to know that if difficulties are identified at an early stage, emotional support, psychoeducation and self-help resources can often be sufficient to prevent them from developing into more serious conditions that require professional input. When intervention is needed, compassion and support at home and in school are hugely important to the process of children and young people overcoming and managing their difficulties.

---

11   Clinical Partners (2021) Treatment for Depression in Teenagers and Children. Available at: https://www.clinical-partners.co.uk/child-adolescents/a-z-of-issues/depression-in-children/treatment-for-depression-in-teenagers-and-children

Chapter 2: Prevalence and provision

Prior to the COVID-19 pandemic, the UK Government's Department of Health and Department for Education conducted several research studies and surveys on the prevalence of mental health problems in our children and young people. A key survey in 2017 revealed the extent and increasing frequency of these difficulties, and a shortfall in the provision and funding of adequate and timely mental health services.[12] A Government Green Paper of the same year reported that a large percentage of young people did not have access to NHS support or treatment, and that the waiting list for one in five children with a referral was in excess of six months.

> **Key Point**
>
> A Government Green Paper of 2017 reported that a large percentage of young people did not have access to NHS support or treatment.

Going forward, an integral part of the Government's plan is to increase and improve the provision of mental health services for children and young people. There is an emphasis on the growing need to support communities, parents, schools and colleges in managing the difficulties that young people are facing. The following areas are regarded as central to successful implementation of the initiatives:

- To recruit and fund a new mental health workforce for community-based support teams, supervised by NHS professionals, specifically for children and young people.
- To provide greater access to NHS mental health services and to reduce waiting times for services for children and young people.
- To ensure that schools have designated lead teachers who are trained in mental health to identify at-risk children and young people. These teachers would oversee the school's pastoral policy and approaches to mental health problems, and develop positive and non-punitive behaviour management policies.

---

12 NHS Digital (2017) *Mental Health of Children and Young People in England, 2017*. Available at: https://digital.nhs.uk/data-and-information/publications/statistical/mental-health-of-children-and-young-people-in-england/2017/2017

- To ensure the earliest possible intervention and prevention of mental health difficulties. This would involve education for schools and parents on the warning signs that a young person may be struggling with anxiety or depression.
- To provide teachers with clear signposting and referral guidelines, and appropriate contact numbers. There is a need for adequate resources to support young people at home and in school if onward referral is not considered necessary.
- To offer comprehensive guidance for schools on how they can work towards providing compassionate, inclusive and supportive learning environments.[13]

The impact of the COVID-19 pandemic

In July 2020, a survey was carried out by the NHS to examine changes in the mental health of children and young people in England since 2017. The resulting report found that one in six children aged five to sixteen (16.0%) were identified as having a probable mental disorder, up from one in nine (10.8%) in 2017. The increase was evident in both boys and girls. The report also considered the influence of the COVID-19 pandemic on the lives of families, and in particular the anxiety and emotional problems triggered by this unprecedented world health crisis. It was found that children and adolescents with a probable pre-existing mental condition were much more likely to have become anxious about the global pandemic.[14]

Studies suggest that additional research is needed to fully understand the effects of the COVID-19 world health crisis. This is vital to mitigate emerging problems, and to identify where help is most needed. It has been shown that the mental health of pre-adolescent children was negatively impacted by COVID-19. Moreover, children and young people with special educational needs and/or neurodevelopmental difficulties developed increased symptoms of mental health problems during the pandemic.[15]

---

13 Department of Health & Department for Education (2017) *Transforming Children and Young People's Mental Health Provision: a Green Paper.* Available at: https://assets.publishing.service.gov.uk/government/uploads/system/uploads/attachment_data/file/664855/Transforming_children_and_young_people_s_mental_health_provision.pdf

14 NHS Digital (2020) *Mental Health of Children and Young People in England, 2020: Wave 1 follow up to the 2017 survey.* Available at: https://digital.nhs.uk/data-and-information/publications/statistical/mental-health-of-children-and-young-people-in-england/2020-wave-1-follow-up

15 Waite P, Pearcey S, Shum A, Raw J, Patalay P & Creswell C (2020) *How did the mental health of children and adolescents change during early lockdown during the COVID-19 pandemic in the UK?* Available at: https://doi.org/10.31234/osf.io/t8rfx

In January 2021, YoungMinds, a UK mental health charity for children and young people, conducted the fourth in a series of surveys exploring the impact of the COVID-19 pandemic and involving 2,438 young people aged between thirteen and twenty-five. It found that the succession of lockdowns had been emotionally difficult, causing high levels of anxiety, low mood and distress. This was particularly pronounced in those who had already been struggling with mental health issues and negative life events. The main causes for concern were loneliness, lack of normal structure and routine, isolation from friends, worries about academic progress and uncertainty about the future. 67% of the subjects felt that the pandemic was likely to affect their mental health in the longer term, particularly those who had gone through bereavements, difficulties in maintaining friendships and setbacks to their educational progress. On a positive note, 79% believed that their emotional wellbeing would improve as restrictions were lifted.

The YoungMinds survey generated a number of recommendations for the UK Government and the Department of Health to ensure recovery:

- Wellbeing should be a priority, and school catch-up planning and implementation need to be in place for children and young people.
- Funding and provision of mental health support in schools is essential.
- It is important to ensure that local charities and youth organisations providing mental health support are maintained.
- Young people must have access to support with clear signposting to mental health provision.[16]

In May 2021, the British Association of Counselling and Psychotherapy (BACP) released a report based on a survey of 4,923 of its members. This recommended that each secondary school, college and academy in the UK should have a dedicated counsellor to help young people cope, recover and thrive following the pandemic. England was found to be behind other UK countries in the provision of mental health staff in schools.[17]

Research continues, and the long-term effects of lockdowns, social distancing, isolation and disruption to education are not yet fully known. While the impact on mental health has been significant for many people, this will hopefully be temporary. However, for those who were already suffering with mental health difficulties, the negative consequences of the

---

16 YoungMinds (2021) *Coronavirus: Impact on young people with mental health needs.* Available at: https://www.youngminds.org.uk/media/esifqn3z/youngminds-coronavirus-report-jan-2021.pdf

17 BACP (2021) *BACP Mindometer report 2021.* Available at: https://www.bacp.co.uk/media/12065/bacp-mindometer-report-2021.pdf

COVID-19 pandemic are likely to be more prolonged.[18] It is hoped that if the Department of Health and Department for Education act according to the recommendations above, then the deficits in provision will continue to be addressed and resolved. This will provide adequate levels of support for communities, parents and schools to identify and help children and young people with mental health difficulties. In light of the traumatic and detrimental impact of the pandemic, this is needed now more than ever.

---

18 Centre for Mental Health (2020) *Covid-19 and the nation's mental health. Forecasting needs and risks in the UK*. Available at: https://www.centreformentalhealth.org.uk/sites/default/files/2020-05/CentreforMentalHealth_COVID_MH_Forecasting_May20.pdf

Chapter 3: Causes and consequences

The onset of mental health difficulties in children and young people can be due to a combination of many factors including genetics, biology, individual temperament and environmental influences.[19] Adverse life events and neurodevelopmental differences can also play a role. For the genetic and biological component, research has demonstrated that children who have one or more family members with anxiety and depression can have a biological vulnerability to inheriting and developing similar temperaments and personality traits. In other words, hereditary levels of biological imbalance in brain chemistry or neurotransmitters can create mood disorders that continue from one generation to the next.

> **Key Point**
>
> Mental health difficulties in children and young people ccan be due to a combination of many factors including genetics, biology, individual temperament and environmental influences.

Moving from 'nature' to 'nurture', a notable influence on the likelihood of children developing anxiety or depression is the possibility of them learning associated behaviours from significant others. For example, they may see a parent with anxiety modelling fearful thinking and emotions or avoidant behaviours in response to stressful situations. This can then be interpreted by the child as the normal and appropriate way to deal with problems.[20]

Environmental factors

Children can develop mental health problems such as anxiety, low self-esteem and depression if they have experienced instability in their home lives while growing up. They may be insecurely attached to their parents or primary carers, which can have an adverse effect on their subsequent social and emotional development.

---

19 Stallard, P. (2009) *Anxiety: Cognitive Behaviour Therapy with Children and Young People.* London: Routledge.

20 Pereira, A.I., Barros, L., Mendonça, D. & Muris. P. (2013) The relationships among parental anxiety, parenting, and children's anxiety: The mediating effects of children's cognitive vulnerabilities. *Journal of Child and Family Studies* 23 (2) 399-409.

The establishment of an emotional bond and secure attachment to a parent or primary caregiver is vitally important for the healthy psychological development of children. The key figures in the development of attachment theory, John Bowlby and Mary Ainsworth, proposed that if a child's primary carer is attuned and responsive to their needs, then the child will feel safe and secure in the world and be less vulnerable to emotional difficulties.[21] Secure attachment develops when primary caregivers are consistently nurturing, protective and dependable, and emotionally connected to a child. This kind of healthy and adaptive bond provides a base from which they can confidently explore and learn about the outside world, happy in the knowledge that they can return to the protection and safety of that relationship and have their emotional and basic needs met.[22]

Young people are less susceptible to anxiety and depression when they have a secure base and a nurturing relationship with their primary caregivers. They feel cared for, protected, valued and supported. Children need to have people they can depend upon and trust to turn to at difficult times in their lives. If they have had solid attachment bonds with their parent or caregiver, they tend to have good levels of self-esteem and confidence. Usually, these individuals will find it easy to trust others and form good relationships, and they will have a positive sense of themselves. They are likely to be independent and able to cope with challenges, and to generally achieve well. Secure attachments both at home and at school are important foundations for the wellbeing and resilience of children.

Unfortunately, if a parent or primary caregiver is struggling with their own mental health, they may not have the capacity to be emotionally available for their child or respond sufficiently to their needs. These difficulties can lead to insecure attachment. In many cases, the parent may not have had healthy attachment relationships in their own childhood, and as a result they may not be aware of their importance and benefits. They can therefore have difficulty with parenting and establishing secure bonds. Promisingly, however, parent-child attachment difficulties can be assessed and improved with the help of mental health professionals and parental training. Foster carers and adoptive parents can also benefit from these therapeutic interventions when they are working towards establishing positive relationships with children and young people who have attachment difficulties and behavioural issues.

---

21 Ainsworth, M.D.S. & Bowlby, J. (1991) An ethological approach to personality development. *American Psychologist* 46 (4) 333-341.
22 Maslow, A.H. (1943) A Theory of Human Motivation. *Psychological Review* 50 (4), 430-437.

Neurodevelopmental differences

Having a neurodevelopmental difference such as autism, ADHD or dyslexia can unfortunately predispose some children and young people to anxiety and low mood. Life can be difficult for these individuals. They may struggle if they feel different from their peers. They can interpret themselves in a negative way, and this can result in emotional difficulties and low self-esteem. They can, however, thrive and do well in life if we are mindful of their wellbeing and ensure that they are given appropriate attention and support. The National Institute for Health Care and Excellence has published helpful guidelines on the management of mental health problems for people with learning disabilities, which can be accessed online.[23]

Life changes and adverse events

Things that happen in a child or young person's life can be stressful, traumatic and difficult to manage.[19] Life changes are one of the most significant causes of anxiety and mood difficulties, and they can affect individuals in different ways. Depending on their past experiences and temperament, what one young person copes with well another may find emotionally distressing. Life changes can create worries and fears about the unknown, and uncertainty and uneasiness around the possibility of things not going well. Most children and young people go through many challenging transitions in their school lives – such as starting school, changing year or transferring from one educational setting to another.

Jennifer Allen and Ron Rapee at the Centre for Emotional Health, MacQuarie University, Australia, developed a Child and Adolescent Survey of Experiences[24] to assess the impact of positive and negative childhood and adolescent life experiences. They included a number of events and changes that can cause anxiety and emotional difficulties, such as:

- moving to a new house
- parental separation or divorce
- parents seeing someone new
- parent being away from their home overnight
- parent adjusting to a new job or losing their job
- a person they care about moving away

---

23 NICE (2016) *Mental health problems in people with learning disabilities: prevention, assessment and management*. Available at: https://www.nice.org.uk/guidance/ng54

24 Allen, J., Rapee, R. & Sandberg, S. (2012). Assessment of maternally reported life events in children and adolescents: A comparison of interview and checklist methods. *Journal of Psychopathology and Behavioral Assessment*, 34, 204-215.

- illness in the family
- bereavement in the family
- a member of the family being hurt or injured
- a new baby on the way
- a new person living in the home
- loss or fear of loss of a pet
- witnessing something bad happening
- home being burgled or broken into
- serious family arguments or disputes
- peer friendship issues
- romantic relationships and breakups
- school issues
- poor academic performance
- exam pressures
- parents involved in school issues

Chapter 4: Identifying problems

Children and young people's views

It is essential to understand what children and young people themselves see as important for maintaining their happiness and good mental health. In October 2020, the Office for National Statistics published the results of a research study involving ten focus groups of children aged ten to fifteen from England, Northern Ireland, Scotland and Wales.[25] The young people were asked about things that they felt were important for their happiness, resilience and wellbeing. These included:

- having supportive, consistent and reliable people to talk to
- feeling loved
- having supportive, positive and caring relationships – particularly with their family and friends
- feeling safe in their home and other environments
- having safe places to spend time in with their friends, which were lacking in some neighbourhoods
- being able to be their authentic selves without judgement
- feeling safe in school
- feeling safe online
- not having a strain on family finances, which can impact negatively on social inclusion
- living in a country that is at peace and where children's needs are important to society and decision-making authorities
- feeling that they could have a voice in decisions which affect them

These are clearly protective factors and pre-requisites for contentment and healthy emotional and social development, and we will explore some of them further in later chapters.

---

[25] Office for National Statistics (2020) *Children's views on well-being and what makes a happy life, UK*. Available at: https://www.ons.gov.uk/peoplepopulationandcommunity/wellbeing/articles/childrensviewsonwellbeingandwhatmakesahappylifeuk2020/2020-10-02

Understanding mental health problems

Sensing that a child or young person is experiencing emotional difficulties can cause great concern for parents and teachers alike. When we witness signs of distress, we can often feel ill-equipped to offer support and may avoid or delay intervening. We may fear that we will do the wrong thing or worsen the situation. However, when we educate ourselves and understand more about the nature of anxiety and depression, we can become more confident to reach out and be of help.

> ## Key Point
> *When we educate ourselves about the nature of anxiety and depression, we can feel more confident to reach out and offer support.*

Due to the amount of time parents and teachers spend with children and teenagers, they are in a position to have a very positive and constructive impact. To begin with, it is important to learn about the characteristics and indicators of anxiety and depression. It is not unusual for these problems to coexist, and a combination of symptoms and behaviours from both conditions may be present.

Indicators of anxiety[26]

- not coping well with change
- sleep disturbance
- bad dreams
- seeming on edge and unsettled
- difficulties with concentration
- changes in appetite
- flare-ups of frustration and irritability
- uncharacteristic tearfulness
- unusual angry outbursts
- preoccupation with lots of fearful thoughts and worries
- withdrawing and ruminating
- avoidance of change and trying out new things
- needing to go to the toilet often
- panic attacks
- clingy behaviour
- complaining of feeling unwell and physical symptoms such as nausea, stomach aches or headaches

---

26 NHS (2020) *Signs of an anxiety disorder.* Available at: https://www.nhs.uk/mental-health/feelings-symptoms-behaviours/feelings-and-symptoms/anxiety-disorder-signs/

Indicators of depression[27]

- feeling down and sad most of the time
- preoccupation with and verbalisation of negative thoughts
- hopelessness
- suicidal or self-harming ideation or actions
- appearing low in confidence
- talking about feelings of low self-worth
- appearing emotionless
- being easily annoyed or irritated
- withdrawing socially from friends and family
- lacking interest in activities they enjoyed previously
- lacking in energy, acting lethargically
- disturbance of sleep patterns – sleeping more or less than usual
- disturbance of eating patterns – eating more or less than usual
- gaining or losing noticeable amounts of weight
- poor concentration and inability to relax
- finding it hard to make decisions
- engaging in unhelpful coping strategies such as use of alcohol/drugs

Challenges for parents and school staff

When supporting a young person with anxiety or depression, parents and school staff may encounter various challenges. They may not know how best to support the young person, the most appropriate ways in which to offer help, or how to provide the secure, supportive and compassionate environments that offer the best chance of recovery. There is also a risk of misinterpreting anxious or depressed behaviours, and mental health disorders that require support going undiagnosed as a result. The teenage brain faces a bombardment of internal and external challenges as part of adolescent cognitive, social and emotional development, and this can spill over into emotions and behaviours, so understanding development and life changes in children and young people is essential. Further information about the teenage brain and mood difficulties can be found in Chapter 24.

Even when problems are identified, knowing whether clinical intervention is required – and if so, who to turn to – can be difficult. The protocols for ascertaining whether family and school support is

---

27 NHS (2020) *Depression in children and young people.* Available at: https://www.nhs.uk/mental-health/children-and-young-adults/advice-for-parents/children-depressed-signs/

sufficient, or if there is a need for onward referral, are often unclear, causing concern and confusion for teachers and parents. In addition, there are factors and barriers that can make it difficult for children and teenagers to ask for support – for example, if they are emotionally incapacitated or fearful of the stigma that they believe will be associated with having psychological difficulties. In this respect, ensuring the provision of a school curriculum that fosters emotional wellbeing and normalises mental health difficulties is vital.

Andrew Garner, an expert on early brain development and the effects of stress and trauma, emphasises how important it is for parents and carers to be vigilant of the signs of emotional problems in children and young people, even if they are not directly related to neurological development:

> *"As long as teenagers are social, eating and sleeping well, and working towards the fulfilment of their plan (for most, good grades leading to college), then I'm happy and their parents should be happy, too. If, on the other hand, they are withdrawn or acting out, not eating, or sleeping regularly, or are letting their grades or dreams pass them by, then I encourage the parents to sound the alarm and get some help."*[28]

---

28 Healthy Children (2019) *What's Going on in the Teenage Brain?* Available at: https://www.healthychildren.org/English/ages-stages/teen/Pages/Whats-Going-On-in-the-Teenage-Brain.aspx

Ten key things to know about anxiety and depression

1. Anxiety and depression are common, highly treatable mental health difficulties that can affect children and young people.

2. Anxiety and depression can coexist at the same time.

3. The onset of anxiety or depression can be due to a combination of many factors including genetic, temperament and environment.

4. The COVID-19 pandemic has been emotionally difficult for young people, and its long-term effects are not yet clearly understood.

5. Early intervention and prevention of problems is critical to managing anxiety and depression.

6. Anxiety and depression can be overcome with support from parents and educators, in addition to therapeutic treatment if necessary.

7. Mental health awareness and psychoeducation can enable early detection of problems, preventing more serious issues developing.

8. Educating young people about mood difficulties and normalising their experiences can bring significant relief and understanding.

9. Communication and collaboration between parents, teachers and mental health professionals can help to achieve positive outcomes.

10. It is vitally important for parents and carers to maintain their own well-being and to seek support from professionals as required.

Part 2: Contexts and approaches for support

Chapter 5: Where to begin

If your child or teenager has been suffering with anxiety or low mood for a long period, they will most likely be experiencing a mixture of challenging thoughts, emotions and bodily symptoms. They may be feeling emotionally drained and hopeless, isolate themselves from other people, and withdraw from the things that

> *Key Point*
>
> *If the anxiety or depression has reached a point where you are feeling overwhelmed, it is important to seek professional support.*

they once took part in and enjoyed. You might have a good idea of what is troubling them if you are aware of any difficulties they are facing, such as life changes, problems within the family, friendship issues, bullying or struggles with schoolwork.

There are many ways in which you can help a young person to break unhelpful cycles of anxiety and low mood. You can talk to them and be at their side when emotions are distressing and overwhelming, and you can help them to adopt practical coping strategies for all aspects of their emotional challenges. However, if the anxiety or depression has reached a point where you are finding it difficult to help and are feeling overwhelmed yourself, it is important to reach out to professionals who are trained and experienced in therapeutic work. It is also vital that you take care of yourself and draw upon your own sources of support, such as friends and family.

Looking after yourself

Being a parent can be rewarding but it is not always easy, particularly if your son or daughter is displaying distressed behaviour. It is important to step back and avoid feeling responsible or that you are not a good parent. It is often very hard to know where to begin to help your child. If you need to seek assistance from a professional, their purpose is not to judge you but to support you in helping the young person you care for to recover. By virtue of reaching out, you are clearly demonstrating your love and concern. It can also alleviate some of the pressure you may be feeling.

Be kind to yourself. If you are struggling, self-care and support are essential. It is often a good idea to have a trusted person you can talk to. Your GP should be able to help with a referral to talking therapy if things become overwhelming. Asking for help is a sign of strength, and it will be seen as such. Draw upon resources such as the help of friends and family so that you can put in place some protected time for yourself. This doesn't have to be excessive, but it is important to find opportunities to relax, exercise, socialise and do things that you enjoy.

It may also be helpful to contact the school to let them know that your child is struggling, and to ask for support if you are comfortable doing so. You could share your concerns with the class teacher, headteacher or head of year. If there is a school counsellor or psychologist, make an appointment to speak with them. It can be hugely beneficial for children and young people to feel that they have support both at home and in school. If parents and teachers have a shared understanding of what the individual is going through, this can be an essential foundation for their recovery.[29]

Coping strategies and techniques to alleviate anxiety and low mood

If you see a child or young person struggling with emotional difficulties, reach out to them. Be clear that it is not unusual to experience challenging and intense emotions when life feels tough and problems seem impossible to overcome. Show concern, and demonstrate that you take what they are experiencing seriously. Let them know that there are ways in which you can help them cope, and that sharing problems can bring relief and perspective.

Explain to the young person that there are many strategies to help them with how they are feeling. A wide range of evidence-based coping techniques are available, but keep in mind that one size does not fit all. It is important to help each child or young person to try out several different strategies to determine which they prefer and which they find most effective. If emotional difficulties are identified at an early stage, parents and teachers can use psychoeducation and self-help resources to prevent the development of more chronic anxiety and low mood.

More information on the strategies and principles that can be helpful for anxiety and low mood in young people is set out in the remainder of this Part of the book. Parts 3 and 4 then explore specific types of anxiety and depression, using case examples to look in detail at coping and recovery strategies that have been applied successfully in real-life situations.

---

29 Adapted from YoungMinds: *Parents survival guide*. Available at: www.youngminds.org.uk/parent/survival-guide/

How to help – first aid in times of extreme anxiety or panic

If a young person's anxiety escalates and they lose self-control, the key priority is to manage the situation until the crisis has passed and calm is restored.

☞ Try to stay calm and composed yourself, and speak to the young person in a soothing, comforting tone. Distract them from anxious thoughts by talking about something else.

☞ If there are other people around, find a quiet space to sit together. Some children will appreciate a hug; teenagers may need more space and feel happy just to be in the same room as you. Ask them what they'd like to do, and give them some time on their own if that's what they need. Tell them you're there to talk when they're ready.

☞ Acknowledge how they are feeling. Explain that their symptoms are only temporary, and that panic or anxiety can feel like a wave which rises to a peak but then starts to fall. The physical discomfort that they are currently experiencing will subside naturally in a similar way.

☞ Show them how to take slow, steady breaths to regulate their anxious breathing and feel calmer. Sit with them, counting while they breathe in through the nose for four to five seconds, hold, then exhale through the mouth. It can be helpful to teach them at a time when they are not anxious to imagine that they are breathing in air which is a calm colour and breathing out air that is a negative, stressful colour.

☞ When the child feels more settled, suggest that they choose and visualise a peaceful, safe place where they have felt calm and happy. Encourage them to hold that image and the associated feeling for as long as possible. If a visualisation is too intense or difficult, ask the child to describe what is in the room, for example a picture or object.

When the intensity of emotion has subsided, help the child to select and get absorbed in a soothing and relaxing activity. This could be going for a walk, drawing, listening to favourite music, reading, talking to a friend or playing with the family pet.

 Each child or young person will have their own choices regarding the coping strategies they prefer. When the panic has abated, it is a good idea to encourage them to identify what they feel works best for them and to make a list of strategies that they can call on in times of need.[30]

Five key areas for intervention

When you have learned a little about the nature of anxiety and depression, it becomes much easier to assess a situation and understand how to adopt a constructive approach to helping a young person in their time of need. Throughout the remainder of this book, we will base our support strategy around five key areas for intervention:

1. Adopt and model a calm approach to the situation. Explain to the young person what you know about the problem and how it can feel, and normalise it. Identify the main issues and reasons for their worries.

2. Cultivate emotional awareness. Help the young person to identify and cope with their emotions. Show understanding and validate their feelings.

3. Help the young person to learn and practise self-regulating and soothing coping strategies to manage symptoms. Adopt strategies for general wellbeing.

---

[30] Adapted from YoungMinds: *Supporting your child with anxiety: A guide for parents.* Available at: https://youngminds.org.uk/find-help/for-parents/parents-guide-to-support-a-z/parents-guide-to-support-anxiety/#what-is-anxiety?

4. Help the young person to identify and challenge negative thoughts and worries. Develop alternative, more realistic thoughts and positive self-talk. Speak to them about the link between unhelpful thoughts, emotions and behaviours.

5. Help the young person to recognise and understand any unhelpful and avoidant behaviours. Talk about helping them to reduce symptoms by gradually facing their fears and trying to get back to enjoying life.

These five key areas for effective intervention will be explored in more detail in the chapters that follow. They will also be referred to in Parts 3 and 4, where we will make use of case examples to look in detail at specific forms of anxiety and depression and how to help in real-life situations.

An excellent resource for working with these areas of intervention has been written by Professor Paul Stallard, a clinical psychologist and international expert in Cognitive Behavioural Therapy (CBT). Think Good, Feel Good is an evidence-based CBT workbook devised specifically for children and young people.[31] It is an exceptionally comprehensive tool with an easy-to-understand format, and it is used extensively in mental health clinical practice. It contains psychoeducation and practical, user-friendly worksheets developed for engagement with children and young people struggling with a range of emotional difficulties. In my experience, it is also a most valuable guide for anyone who works with children and young people, such as school nurses, therapists, teachers and parents.

---

31 Stallard, P. (2018) *Think Good, Feel Good: A Cognitive Behavioural Therapy Workbook for Children and Young People, 2nd Edition.* John Wiley and Sons

Chapter 6: Talking about difficult feelings

An important first step in helping a child or young person to cope with emotional difficulties is giving them the opportunity to talk about how they are feeling. Set aside time for this in a quiet place. Try to approach the situation gently and calmly. Normalise anxiety and low mood as difficulties that everyone experiences at times. Adopt and model a matter-of-fact approach to what they are going through and the available methods of coping. Be clear that there are various ways in which you can help.

> ### Expert View
>
> *"I'm not saying to pretend you don't have stress and anxiety, but let kids see you managing it calmly, tolerating it, feeling good about getting through it."*
>
> Dr Clark Goldstein[32]

It is not easy to see a young person in distress. It is important, however, to be aware of your own emotional responses, and to be mindful not to display them. Do your best to be as composed, patient and encouraging as you can. Be open about your own experiences of anxiety and low mood. If you show that you have healthy ways of handling these difficulties, the child can learn how to do the same and will believe that you are able to help them.

Most importantly, emphasise that it can feel so much better to share your worries with someone you trust and think about ways to resolve them than to keep everything to yourself. This will help your child to feel less isolated, and less that they must carry the burden of dealing with their difficulties alone. It is respectful and helpful to ask them what they feel would help. Teenagers may not always want to open up straight away. If they aren't ready, give them space and make sure they know you'll be there when they need you. Many young people communicate via text or other messaging platforms, which could be a good way to check in and let them know that you're thinking of them.

---

[32] Goldstein, C. (2021) *What to Do (and Not Do) When Children Are Anxious*. Available at: https://childmind.org/article/what-to-do-and-not-do-when-children-are-anxious/

Cultivate emotional awareness

Emotional support and secure attachment are important foundations for healthy social and emotional development. Good connections with parents who are emotionally available to their children, and who meet their emotional needs, help young people to develop emotional awareness, empathy, positivity and positive interpersonal relationships.[33]

Encourage your child or teenager to identify and express the unhelpful feelings that they are experiencing. It can be useful to ask them to rate the intensity out of ten, to help you to understand which areas and emotions are most problematic. Be their safe base at a time when life is feeling difficult. Attuning to your child's emotional needs and providing them with nurture, support and attention will help them to feel safe, loved and valued. They will also be more likely to open up to you.

Speaking about what they are experiencing can give the young person a sense of relief and help them to feel understood and less burdened. It can provide hope and encouragement to be brave, and to try to cope with you at their side. They may sometimes find it difficult to talk about and name difficult emotions, and this can take time and patience. Reassure them that you can work together at a pace they can cope with. It is helpful to have an agreed signal that they can use if they need to have a break. Stop for as long as needed, and praise each courageous step they take.

There are many resources available to support children and young people to identify and speak about their feelings. The range of age-appropriate formats includes pictures of faces with feelings written below, printable worksheets, wheels of emotions, emoticons and mood cards. There are also books with pictures and stories about feelings and the benefits of sharing and expressing emotions. Additional ways to explore how someone is feeling include play, games, painting, drawing and crafts.

There is a wealth of websites containing videos, informative guides about anxiety and depression and case studies showing how young people have faced these problems and coped. Norfolk Children and Young People's Services has developed a fantastic resource for talking about difficult feelings. The Just One Norfolk website[34] offers a range of tools for naming and expressing emotions, as well as activities to enhance emotional health and links to other materials. The table below is drawn from this resource.

---

33 Gökçe, G. & Yilmaz, B. (2018). Emotional Availability of Parents and Psychological Health: What Does Mediate This Relationship? *Journal of Adult Development. 25 37-47.*

34 www.justonenorfolk.nhs.uk

How to help – talking about feelings

☞ Resources suitable for working with younger children (available from the Just One Norfolk website[35]):

- **Emotions:** A range of age-appropriate resources to help children identify and explore the emotions they are feeling. There are visuals and pictures of children's faces with various expressions accompanied by explanations of how they feel. The website also provides charts to help them rate the intensity of emotions.
- **Self-confidence and self-esteem:** Tips and activities to help young people think and feel more positively about themselves, and to identify and build on their strengths, confidence and self-esteem.
- **Resilience:** Games and activities that parents can use to engage their child and help them develop resilience for when life is tough.
- **Self-care:** A range of delightful self-nurturing and wellbeing activities and videos for primary and secondary school pupils.
- **Mindfulness:** Apps, breathing and body scan exercise videos, and stress-busting activities.
- **Worries and anxiety:** Advice on how to talk to and support children, how to cope with anxiety, information on emotional regulation, and mindfulness activities to soothe and instil calm.
- **Low mood:** A range of mood-boosting activities including videos on breathing and progressive muscle relaxation, a parent workshop, educational videos, and podcasts on feeling anxious or down.
- **Anger:** Resources to help children talk about what makes them feel angry (which can indicate underlying anxiety) and learn methods for expressing their feelings in more healthy ways.
- **Anti-bullying:** Advice, videos and activities to help parents understand the effects of bullying. There is guidance on how to talk to and support the child, and how to prevent bullying.

---

35 (www.justonenorfolk.nhs.uk/emotional-health/children-young-peoples-emotional-health/emotional-health-activities/feelings-activities)

Resources suitable for older children and teenagers[36]:

- **How to Communicate with Teenagers (Relate):** Advice on how to connect and develop positive relationships with teenagers, and how to communicate with them in appropriate, helpful ways.
- **Talking to Your Teen (NHS):** Guidance on how to encourage teenagers to open up and talk about how they are feeling.
- **Tips for Communicating with Teenagers (Child Mind Institute):** Helpful advice on how to approach teenagers and communicate with them at this sensitive time in their emotional development.
- **Balancing Screen Time (Internet Matters):** Crucial advice for parents and schools on how to strike a healthy balance between life online and offline.
- **Online Safety Advice (Childnet):** Guidance and helpful information about online safety for parents and carers.

---

36 www.justonenorfolk.nhs.uk/childhood-development-additional-needs/talk-play/older-children-and-teens

Chapter 7: Strategies for soothing and self-regulation

If you have recognised that a young person is struggling with anxiety or low mood, it is helpful for them to begin learning coping strategies as soon as possible. Help them practise these techniques at times when they don't feel anxious or low, so they are equipped to call upon them when needed. This usually gives young people a sense that they will be able to cope, helping them to feel more in control and confident when anxiety levels are high.

> **Key Point**
>
> *If you have recognised that your child is struggling with anxiety or low mood, it is helpful for them to begin learning coping strategies as soon as possible.*

Understanding physical symptoms

Explaining to a child that there are a range of bodily sensations that anxious people feel, and identifying what they themselves personally experience when distressed, can help to normalise symptoms. This gives parents and carers a greater understanding of the child's particular responses and indicators of anxiety. It also often enhances the young person's feeling of being understood and supported. They can get a sense of relief from knowing that you are really attuned to them and understand how they feel. Recognising their own bodily signals when they are becoming anxious, and learning effective coping strategies, can also reduce their sense of helplessness and hopelessness and the fear of losing control.

Self-soothing skills and techniques

The emotional and physical symptoms of anxiety and depression can be relieved and reduced if we learn self-soothing skills and relaxation techniques. These include breathing training, progressive muscle relaxation and visualisations. Your child or teenager may find them easier with the aid of guided audio tracks, and there are many resources available including apps and age-appropriate CDs. It is a good idea to sample these together to find out what your child prefers.

By practising these self-soothing skills when they are not experiencing high levels of distress, children and young people can have effective tools at their disposal for when they feel anxious or overwhelmed. These are skills for life, and they will promote positive emotions and general wellbeing. It is very important to find what works best for the individual, and different strategies will be appropriate depending on what they are experiencing in the moment. The skills can be explored, practised and mastered together. Alternatively, if they prefer, the young person can read through this part of the book and try out the techniques independently.

An effective way of helping your child or teenager to overcome anxiety and low mood is to emphasise the importance of being as compassionate and kind to themselves as they would be towards friends and other people they care about. This can help them to adopt a supportive and gentle mindset, rather than judging themselves negatively because they are struggling with mental health difficulties. It is normal to experience anxiety or low mood, and human beings sometimes need a little help to overcome it. This is a hugely important step on the road to recovery.

Diaphragmatic deep breathing

High levels of anxiety can cause rapid breathing and affect our ability to inhale as deeply and evenly as we normally would. We can feel that we are unable to breathe properly, and this can trigger a 'fight or flight' response. If there is an imbalance in our levels of oxygen and carbon dioxide, and we are breathing out too much carbon dioxide, this can result in light-headedness, muscle tension, headaches, and feeling shaky or unsteady. Hyperventilation and shallow breathing can feel exhausting and alarming, exacerbate anxiety and cause panic. However, these are usually temporary sensations and it is important to remember that they are not necessarily dangerous.

Slowing down and regulating the rate of our breathing can reduce anxiety, help to create a sense of calm, and ease fearful or racing thoughts. It also releases endorphins in the brain, which has a calming effect and can help with anxiety and low mood. If we are caught in a cycle of shallow breathing, endorphin release does not occur. Further benefits of deep breathing include the promotion of improved sleep and concentration[37] – as well as regulation of the heart rate, bringing it more in sync with the breath. The technique for this is quite easy to learn and perform.

---

37 Perciavalle, V., Blandini, M., Fecarotta, P., Buscemi, A., Di Corrado, D., Bertolo, L., Fichera, F. & Coco, M.(2017) The role of deep breathing on stress. *Neurological Sciences* 38: 451-458.

How to help – diaphragmatic deep breathing

If you practise diaphragmatic deep breathing with your child or teenager, you can reap the benefits for yourself too. This self-soothing technique can be a fun and bonding exercise to do together.

☞ Pick a quiet time of day and find a place to sit or lie comfortably without being disturbed.

☞ Inhale slowly through your nose for a count of four seconds. Try to breathe deeply right down into your stomach. This can be easier if you place your hand on your abdomen. You will be able to feel it rising as you breathe in and falling as you breathe out.

☞ Hold that breath for a count of three or four seconds.

☞ Exhale and release the breath through the nose for about six seconds.

☞ Pause and begin to inhale again, then repeat the process.

It is best to practise diaphragmatic deep breathing when you are not feeling anxious or agitated. Ideally, make time to regulate and slow down the breath once or twice a day. This technique helps people to reduce levels of anxiety in the moment, and to feel more in control of associated bodily symptoms. Once you have learned the skill, you can use it discreetly at any time without drawing attention to yourself.

Progressive muscle relaxation

Progressive muscle relaxation involves learning to tense and relax groups of muscles in order to release tension in our bodies. This is quite easy to do, and it is an excellent way to soothe the body and mind by creating a sense of calm and wellbeing. It can promote both psychological and physiological states of relaxation.[38]

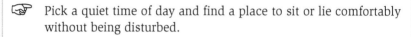 How to help – progressive muscle relaxation

☞ Pick a quiet time of day and find a place to sit or lie comfortably without being disturbed.

☞ Tighten the areas listed below, hold for ten seconds, then relax. Some people like to say the word 'relax' to themselves as they do this.

- Squeeze your fists for about ten seconds and then release.
- Tighten all the muscles along your arms and then relax them.
- Push your shoulders back and up towards the ceiling, then relax.
- Tighten your stomach muscles as much as you can and release.
- Tighten all the muscles in your legs and release.
- Curl your toes and hold them tight, then release.
- Squeeze the muscles in your face and then relax.

☞ When you have finished, notice how your body feels and try to stay in this relaxed state for as long as you can.

---

38 Toussaint, L., Nguyen, Q.A., Roettger, C., Dixon, K., Offenbächer, M., Kohls, N., Hirsch, J. & Sirois, F. (2021). Effectiveness of Progressive Muscle Relaxation, Deep Breathing, and Guided Imagery in Promoting Psychological and Physiological States of Relaxation. *Evidence-Based Complementary and Alternative Medicine* 5924040.

Guided visualisations

Another excellent way to relax, reduce stress and soothe anxious thoughts is to listen to guided visualisations of positive imagery. This can take the mind to a calm and peaceful place, away from everyday stress, tension and worries. There are many recordings of guided meditations available that conjure up settings such as tropical beaches or beautiful gardens. We can even create our own peaceful imagery if we have a particular memory of a place where we have felt calm, tranquil and safe, and visualise this place whenever we feel the need to relax and reduce stress levels.

How to help – visualising a safe and happy place

☞ Close your eyes and take some calm breaths.

☞ Picture yourself in a place where you have felt happy and safe, or where have been doing something that you really love.

☞ Use all your senses to imagine the place fully. Focus on the fine details – what can you see, hear, smell or taste?

☞ Remember how calm and content you feel in your chosen place. Try to hold onto these sensations for as long as you can.

☞ Stay in your seat for a little while until you come around to the present and feel grounded.

☞ Remember that you can return to this place in your mind whenever you need to – it is your special place

Chapter 8: Sleeping, eating and physical self-care

Our physical and emotional wellbeing are closely connected, and there is growing evidence that physical activity can have a positive impact on low mood and anxiety in children and young people.[39] Regular exercise can be hugely beneficial for our mental health, and recent neurobiological studies have also shown that, in the longer term, exercise can help significantly with negative ways of thinking and mental health problems in young people.[40]

> **Key Point**
>
> There is growing evidence that physical activity can have a positive impact on low mood and anxiety in children and young people.

Exercise can boost our energy and mood, and we often get a great sense of achievement when we choose this as a strategy to help us when feeling low or anxious. If anxiety levels are high and persistent, physical activity, playing sports and getting outdoors can be great ways to shake off nervous energy and feel uplifted. Ensuring that our bodies are healthy makes us better able to cope with problems and emotional difficulties when they arise.

Get enough sleep

The benefits of good-quality sleep cannot be underestimated. Sleep directly affects our mental and physical health and how well we feel during the day. If you are sleeping too much, or not getting enough sleep and need to nap in the daytime, it is important to try to establish a good sleep routine. Sleep that is insufficient or of poor quality can have detrimental effects on concentration and memory. We can feel irritable and low, and become less able to cope with daily functioning. In fact, research has found a correlation between reduced hours

---

39 Carter, T., Pascoe, M., Bastounis, A., Morres, I., Callaghan, P. & Parker, A. (2021) The effect of physical activity on anxiety in children and young people: a systematic review and meta-analysis. *Journal of Affective Disorders* 285 10-21.

40 Heinze, K., Cumming, J., Dosanjh, A., Palin, S., Poulton, S., Bagshaw, A.P. & Broome, M.R. (2021) Neurobiological evidence of longer-term physical activity interventions on mental health outcomes and cognition in young people: A systematic review of randomised controlled trials. *Neuroscience and biobehavioral reviews* 120 431–441.

of sleep and severe mental health difficulties such as anxiety and emotional problems in young people. Parental intervention is advised if this appears to be an issue.[41]

Spending a lot of time on social media has been linked to sleep problems. It can be addictive for children and teenagers, and they often spend time online rather than getting their sufficient quota of rest. Parents should be vigilant of this and set boundaries around screen time. Social media will be discussed further in relation to depression in Chapter 26.

How to help – establishing good sleep habits

The Centre for Clinical Interventions in Australia provides a very helpful guide to improving sleep and establishing a healthy bedtime routine.[42] Its recommendations include:

☞ Go to bed and get up at more or less the same time every day; even at weekends and during holidays.

☞ Only try to sleep when you are actually feeling tired and sleepy.

☞ If you can't sleep after twenty minutes or so, get up and do something relaxing until you feel sleepy.

☞ Avoid naps to ensure that you feel tired at bedtime.

☞ Make sure your bed and bedroom are quiet and comfortable.

☞ Create some bedtime rituals such as stretching or breathing to remind your body that it is time to sleep.

☞ Try keeping a sleep diary for a few weeks to identify your habits.

---

41 Sarchiapone, M., Mandelli, L., Carli, V., Iosue, M., Wasserman, C., Hadlaczky, G., Hoven, C.W., Apter, A., Balazs, J., Bobes, J., Brunner, R., Corcoran, P., Cosman, D., Haring, C., Kaess, M., Keeley, H., Keresztény, A., Kahn, J.P., Postuvan, V., Mars, U., Saiz, P.A., Varnik, P., Sisask, M. & Wasserman, D. (2014) Hours of sleep in adolescents and its association with anxiety, emotional concerns, and suicidal ideation. *Sleep medicine* 15 (2) 248–254.

42 Centre for Clinical Interventions (2021) *Sleep hygiene*. Available at: https://www.cci.health.wa.gov.au/Resources/Looking-After-Yourself/Sleep

Regulate eating problems

There is growing evidence to suggest that a good diet and lifestyle could prevent mental health problems. Moreover, it is emerging that a poor diet can increase the likelihood of depression and anxiety.[43] In 2017 the Mental Health Foundation UK published a research-based booklet entitled *Food for Thought: Mental Health and Nutrition Briefing*, which explains the importance of a well-balanced diet to combat and prevent mental health problems.[44] Holistic mind-body approaches are currently gathering momentum, in addition to thinking around the importance of the interaction between the brain and the gut and the impact this has on mental health and wellbeing.

> ## Expert View
>
> *"There is growing evidence that nutrition may play an important role in the prevention, development and management of mental health problems."*
>
> Mental Health Foundation UK

As with sleep patterns, a young person's appetite can alter if they are suffering with anxiety or low mood, with the result that they eat too little or too much. Teenagers also tend to have a preference for junk food, and the quality of our nutrition is extremely important. Disturbance in food intake and a poorly-balanced diet can have a huge impact on our energy levels, mood stability and functioning.

---

43 Adan, R., van der Beek, E.M., Buitelaar, J.K., Cryan, J.F., Hebebrand, J., Higgs, S., Schellekens, H. & Dickson, S.L. (2019) Nutritional psychiatry: Towards improving mental health by what you eat. *European neuropsychopharmacology: the journal of the European College of Neuropsychopharmacology* 29 (12), 1321–1332.

44 Mental Health Foundation (2017) *Food for thought: Mental health and nutrition briefing.* Available at: https://www.mentalhealth.org.uk/sites/default/files/food-for-thought-mental-health-nutrition-briefing-march-2017.pdf

How to help – regulating eating problems

 Parents and carers can help to regulate a child or young person's diet in the following ways:

- Agree to have regular meals and snacks to maintain energy.
- Prepare healthy meals that are rich in nutrients, vitamins and Omega-3 fatty acids.
- Include complex carbohydrates to boost serotonin levels and sustain energy.
- Avoid too much sugar, refined carbohydrates, trans fats, saturated fats and high levels of preservatives.

 Certain foods have been found to boost mental health:

- **Salmon:** Omega-3 fatty acids found in salmon are correlated with a decrease in mental health problems, and there is evidence that they can boost memory and learning.
- **Chicken:** Chicken helps the body to produce serotonin, which boosts mood and can help with depression and memory.
- **Whole grains:** Complex carbohydrates such as rice, beans and oats provide consistent sources of energy and balance blood sugar. Whole grains also help the brain absorb tryptophan, an essential amino acid. Eating these along with chicken and turkey can reduce depression and anxiety and improve brain function.
- **Avocados:** Avocados help with memory and concentration, and are protective against strokes.
- **Spinach:** Green and leafy vegetables contain folic acid, which helps with depression, insomnia and dementia.
- **Yoghurt:** Probiotics in yoghurt can help with healthy digestion, which links to stress and anxiety reduction. Yoghurt also contains magnesium and potassium, which are helpful for brain function.
- **Nuts:** Nuts are a rich source of Omega-3 fatty acid and can help combat low mood. Almonds aid production of mood-boosting chemicals such as dopamine. Cashews help with brain function.
- **Olive oil:** There is evidence to suggest that pure, extra virgin olive oil helps with learning and memory.

- **Tomatoes:** Tomatoes contain lycopene, which is a powerful antioxidant that boosts concentration and memory and helps to prevent brain cell damage and disease.
- **Dark chocolate:** Dark chocolate (ideally 85% cocoa or more) contains antioxidants, which can help with brain health, mood and memory.[45]

---

[45] Boyles, O. (2018) *10 Foods that Boost Mental Health*. Available at: https://www.icanotes.com/2018/04/04/10-foods-that-boost-mental-health/

Chapter 9: Relaxation, enjoyment and emotional self-care

Making time to relax is very important for mental health. Put simply, emotional self-care means actively looking after your own feelings. In today's turbulent, unpredictable and stressful world, taking time out to care for your whole self, emotionally as well as physically, has become more important than ever. Nurturing emotions, and taking time to consciously process negative emotions, can help to lower stress, build resilience and boost mood. The Anna Freud National Centre for Children and Families advocates self-care activities to manage mental health, and provides information and a relevant range of ideas on its website.[46]

> **Key Point**
>
> *In today's world, taking time out to care for your whole self, emotionally as well as physically, has become more important than ever.*

A great way to disconnect from worrying thoughts and shift the focus away from anxious feelings and bodily sensations is to get involved in an absorbing activity that you enjoy. This can provide a sense of space and calm, and improve low mood and anxiety. At times when you are feeling very anxious or low, it is best to avoid the instinctive response to lie in bed, pull the covers up over your head and worry. Instead, get up and do an activity that takes your mind off things. You will feel much better for taking action and choosing a more healthy and constructive coping strategy. Realising that you are not imprisoned by your negative thoughts, and that you can choose to act in more positive and helpful ways, can really lift your spirits. It can also help you to feel more confident and in control of your worries.

Detailed below are some relaxing and absorbing activities that you, or a young person you care for, could try out in order to distract the mind from anxieties and worries. You may also have your own ideas to add to the list. Sample a range of activities to find out what works best and takes you (or the young person) to a happier place. You can become

---

[46] Anna Freud National Centre for Children and Families: *Self-care*. Available at: https://www.annafreud.org/on-my-mind/self-care/

quite an expert in choosing and practising the activities that help to take you away from the worries that occupy your mind, and the more you do them, the more able you will feel to cope with times when you feel down or anxious.

How to help – relaxing activities

☞ Listen to happy or soothing music (you could spend time making your own worry-busting playlists) or listen to a podcast.

☞ Re-read a favourite book or magazine, or make time to search out new reading material that appeals to you.

☞ Watch enjoyable TV shows or films (comedies are usually a good choice) or play computer games.

☞ Spend time on creative activities such as writing, baking or cooking, drawing, painting or colouring.

☞ Practise yoga or a musical instrument.

☞ Keep a diary or journal.

☞ Take a bubble bath or a shower, have a pamper night or try out aromatherapy.

☞ Talk to a friend or spend some time with the family pet.

Feeling a sense of achievement

Setting realistic daily goals and achieving them can significantly improve mood and energise the mind and body. When we act purposefully to reach goals that we have set for ourselves, we feel a sense of accomplishment and satisfaction. This naturally releases positive neurochemicals such as serotonin and dopamine, both of which boost mood and happiness. Serotonin enhances and stabilises mood, produces feelings of contentment and wellbeing and can regulate sleep and appetite imbalances. Dopamine gives us pleasurable feelings, brings a sense of achievement and motivates us. These neurotransmitters also help to regulate emotions and aid memory and concentration. It is of huge benefit to our mental health and wellbeing to be aware of this, and to act in a way that naturally produces helpful neurochemicals.

Planning to set and achieve goals does not just have to be about accomplishing necessary tasks, such as schoolwork or jobs around the house. Goals aimed at maintaining a positive mood, such as socialising, connecting with other people or engaging in activities that you enjoy, are equally beneficial. It is good to strike a balance between these when planning. A weekly activity diary or motivator sheet can be very useful for organising your time. This can incorporate all the elements above and provide a concrete plan of self-care goals that can be ticked off when they are achieved. It is best to start with small, realistic and achievable goals that incorporate sociable and enjoyable elements.

Socialising and enjoyment

Anxious and depressed young people often do not want to talk about how they are feeling. It is important to notice this, as they can withdraw and spend time alone with difficult thoughts and emotions. Teenagers tend to retreat to their bedrooms and isolate themselves. They avoid contact for many reasons, and as a result they may miss out on spending time enjoying positive relationships. However, connecting with or helping other people boosts the neurotransmitter oxytocin, which promotes wellbeing and enhances mood. It is good to spend time with other people every day – especially close friends and family, but also people in your local community.

> **Key Point**
>
> *Teenagers tend to avoid contact for many reasons, and as a result they may miss out on spending time enjoying positive relationships.*

The tendency of children and particularly teenagers to shy away from doing things they previously enjoyed when they are feeling anxious or down can create further low mood, compounding the problem. This may affect their energy levels and stop them from having fun. Unfortunately, during these periods they are more likely to do things which are draining rather than energising, and they can become more solitary over time. It is therefore important to be vigilant against this, and to help young people begin to do things they enjoyed before the difficulties arose.

Mindfulness

There is growing evidence to support the efficacy of mindfulness techniques for children and young people. Mindfulness-based interventions are increasing in popularity, and many schools are embracing the practice to help pupils improve their mental health, resilience and wellbeing. Mindfulness is also believed to be effective in enhancing children and young people's self-esteem and cognitive skills, and in improving their academic performance and social and interpersonal functioning.[47]

Mindfulness helps us shift our attention away from being preoccupied with anxious and unhelpful thoughts. We can learn how to pay these thoughts less attention, to tolerate them and to avoid engaging with them or reacting to them in anxious ways. Mindfulness exercises allow us to retrain our minds to focus on the 'here and now' in the present moment, without the distraction and distress of negative thoughts and memories. Mindfulness also embodies the practice of self-compassion and kindness.

How to help – mindfulness practices

There are many ways to practise mindfulness, formally and informally, in order to bring your attention to the present moment. It is a good idea to try out a few different techniques to find which you prefer.

☞ **Mindful breathing:** This involves focusing attention on the breath, and noticing the natural rhythm and sensations as you inhale and exhale.

☞ **Body scan:** This encourages you to scan your body and observe the sensations you feel in each area. You can consciously relax the areas you visit, but simply bringing attention to them often has this effect.

☞ **Meditations or visualisations:** Various types of mindfulness audio meditations are available to guide your practice. Techniques include focusing on a word or mantra, or visualising a place or physical object.

☞ **Mindful eating:** This entails taking time to focus on the act of eating and being fully aware and in the moment. For example thinking about where food has come from and how it is made, experiencing all the sensations you receive through your senses, and listening to your body to understand when you are truly hungry or have had enough to eat.

---

47   Dunning, D.L., Griffiths, K., Kuyken, W., Crane, C., Foulkes, L., Parker, J. & Dalgleish, T. (2019) Research Review: The effects of mindfulness-based interventions on cognition and mental health in children and adolescents - a meta-analysis of randomized controlled trials. *Journal of Child Psychology and Psychiatry, and allied disciplines* 60 (3) 244–258.

> ☞ **Mindful walking:** A form of moving meditation in which you tune in to the sensations in your body and the environment as you walk.
>
> ☞ **Mindful artwork:** Making art with a sense of curiosity and freedom, maintaining a conscious awareness of the colours, textures and sounds of what you are creating in the moment. The emphasis is on process rather than outcome, and on experiencing all the senses.

Mindfulness offers many benefits for the young. The practice can enhance concentration as it activates and strengthens the thinking part of the brain. It promotes calm, reflective awareness, and an improved ability to focus and pay attention. Young people are often less impulsive, and more able to regulate their emotions and behaviour. From a physical point of view, mindfulness can help to boost relaxation and alleviate the bodily symptoms of stress. It also improves sleep quality, supporting day to day functioning.

Young people who practice mindfulness tend to feel more positive as they learn how to cope with difficult emotions and let go of negative thoughts. They function better without being overwhelmed by anxiety. Mindfulness also helps to build self-esteem and raise mood, helping children to develop resilience and a 'can do' approach to difficulties. They grow in confidence as they learn to respond positively to situations that they find stressful.

Chapter 10: Challenging unhelpful thoughts

If you are helping a young person to cope with emotional difficulties, encourage them to express their worries and challenge unhelpful ways of thinking. The key factor here is that often there is no foundation for these negative thoughts. They convince us that things are worse than they really are, and if we are struggling with anxiety or low mood then it is easy to have absolute belief in them. However, in reality these thoughts are not necessarily supported by evidence. They can and should be reality-checked and challenged if they are not an accurate reflection of what is happening.

Expert View

"The moods we experience often depend upon our thoughts. Different interpretations of an event can lead to different moods."

Dennis Greenberger and Christine A. Padesky[48]

Negative thinking styles

Set out below are the most common negative thinking styles that young people may develop when they are feeling anxious or depressed.[49,50] Everyone naturally engages in these unhelpful ways of thinking and interpreting events at times. However, if an individual is automatically and frequently thinking in these ways, it can have a detrimental impact on their emotions, behaviour and psychological wellbeing.

Predicting the worst and catastrophising

Anxiety and low mood can cause us to engage in 'what if' thinking that involves excessive worry or rumination. We predict that the worst possible things are going to happen, even when there is little or no evidence that this will be the case. We can get things out of proportion, overestimating how bad we will feel in reality and underestimating our ability to cope.

---

48 Greenberger, D. & Padesky, C.A. (2016) *Mind over mood: Change how you feel by changing the way you think*. New York, NY: Guilford Press.
49 Beck, A.T., Rush, A.J., Shaw, B.F. & Emery, G. (1979) *Cognitive Therapy of Depression*. New York, NY: Guilford Press.
50 Burns, D. (1989) *The Feeling Good Handbook*. New York, NY: Harper-Collins Publishers.

These catastrophic thoughts can occur if we are uncertain about what might happen. We believe that it is helpful to worry in advance and predict how things will turn out and how we could cope. It is important to notice and remember when things do not work out as badly as we predicted, and to recognise that the worries we had were futile and a waste of time.

> Example: You are moving to a new school:
> *"What if people don't like me? I will have no friends, it will be a disaster and I will fall apart."*

Emotional reasoning

Emotional reasoning involves the belief that if you feel anxiety or have an anxious symptom, there must be something to worry about and bad things might happen. However, emotions are just feelings; they are not facts. It is best not to let them guide your sense of reality.

> Example: *"I'm feeling anxious, so something bad is probably going to happen."*

Fortune-telling

When we are feeling anxious or low, we often predict that bad things are going to happen.

> Example: *"I will not do well in my exams and I will never get a good job. I will be a failure."*

Mind-reading

When we are experiencing emotional difficulties, we can believe that we know what others are thinking about us. Rationally, we understand that this is impossible. However, these kinds of thoughts can occupy our minds and cause upset and anxiety.

> Examples: *"They are looking at me and thinking I'm stupid and weird."*
>
> *"The girls in my class think I'm boring."*

Black-and-white thinking

Also referred to as 'all-or-nothing' or dichotomous thinking, this involves thinking in extremes or opposites with no grey areas in between. We interpret a situation as either really good or really bad – a success or a failure. In reality, it may be something that did not go well on one occasion and can be improved upon. This way of thinking is self-defeating and can become generalised to many situations. It can become increasingly intense if it is not recognised and reality-checked.

>Examples: *"I've eaten junk food today, so I have completely ruined my plans to eat healthily."*
>
>*"I have not performed perfectly and so I have totally failed."*
>
>*"If some of the people in my group don't like me, then I'm totally unpopular."*

Overgeneralising

If a particular thing does not go well on one occasion, anxiety or low mood can cause us to think that it is never going to go well.

>Examples: You meet a new teacher who is not nice:
>*"All my new teachers will be horrible."*
>
>Your girlfriend breaks up with you:
>*"I can never keep a girlfriend. They will all dump me."*
>
>You didn't pass one exam:
>*"I will fail everything."*

Negative bias and filtering

Having a negative bias entails focusing solely on the negative aspects of a situation and discounting or filtering out the positive aspects. We tend to only notice the things that have not gone well, and we overlook or ignore the things that have gone to plan or turned out positively.

>Example: One person looked bored while you were speaking, so:
>*"Everyone hated my presentation."*
>
>(Filtering out positive responses, such as the fact that others in the group were nodding attentively.)

Personalising

Personalising in the context of anxiety and depression means believing that the world revolves around us, or that we have more influence on events and others than is really the case. For example, if we are feeling anxious or low, we might assume responsibility and blame ourselves for something that was not completely our fault.

> Examples: *"The group presentation didn't go well just because of me."*
>
> *"My girlfriend finished with me because I'm shy."*

Blaming and not taking responsibility

At the other end of the spectrum from personalisation, anxiety or depression may cause us to blame someone else for our negative behaviour, and refuse to accept responsibility for our own actions.

> Examples: *"They made me feel angry."*
>
> *"I did badly in my exams because the teacher is useless."*

Shoulds and musts, and conditions of worth

Emotional difficulties can sometimes mean that we demand unrealistically high standards of ourselves and others. We put pressure on ourselves regarding how we should or must be as a person. We may feel that we are only a worthwhile or good person if we live up to these standards by consistently behaving and performing well. We might also judge our worth according to our ability to maintain these standards. This perfectionist style of thinking is unhelpful and self-defeating, and it can cause feelings of disappointment in ourselves and others.

> Examples: *"I shouldn't get anxious or depressed."*
>
> *"I should be able to cope with this."*
>
> *"I should work hard always and do well in my exams."*
>
> *"I'm not good enough if I don't perform as well as I should."*
>
> *"I shouldn't ever feel angry."*
>
> *"I should be much thinner than I am."*

Self-criticism and labelling

If we are struggling with challenging emotions, we may naturally think negatively about ourselves and label ourselves critically. Negative self-evaluation can be incredibly unhelpful and damage our self-esteem if it goes unchecked. We can begin to feel worthless because we are being so harsh and unkind to ourselves.

>Examples: *"I'm useless and pathetic."*
>
>*"I'm not worth knowing."*

Comparing and despairing

Comparing ourselves to others is natural to some extent, and it forms part of general teenage self-consciousness. However, constantly judging our appearance, abilities and worth in comparison to other people can be unhealthy and damaging to our confidence and self-esteem.

Social media is a particularly problematic area for young people. It can cause them to feel that others are better in many ways, resulting in continued anxiety and personal dissatisfaction. Extensive use of social media can have an impact on young people's mental health.

In my own experience of working with anxious or depressed young people, over-exposure to social media platforms such as Instagram, Snapchat and Twitter appears to have a detrimental impact on their self-esteem. It also seems to increase self-criticism and compare-and-despair ways of thinking.

>Examples: *"She is much prettier than me."*
>
>*"He is more confident than me."*
>
>*"They do much better in exams than me."*

How to help – challenging unhelpful thoughts

Here are some questions to ask when identifying and challenging worries and negative thoughts.[51] They can help you to find more balanced and realistic alternatives.

☞ What are you thinking and predicting will go wrong?

☞ Could you be catastrophising or thinking in distorted ways (for example fortune-telling, mind-reading or black-and-white thinking)?

☞ Do you believe that your thoughts are facts? Is there evidence to show that this is true? Is there any evidence against it?

☞ How sure are you out of ten that this will happen? In reality, how likely is it to happen?

☞ Has it happened before now?

☞ What's the worst thing that could happen?

☞ If this did happen, is it possible that you would cope with it?

☞ If a good friend was thinking in this way, what do you think you might say to him or her?

☞ Are you using emotional reasoning? Do you think because you are feeling a bit anxious or low that something bad is going to happen?

---

51 Getselfhelp: *Unhelpful Thinking Habits*. Available at: http://www.getselfhelp.co.uk/unhelpful.htm

Dealing with negative thoughts

Worry Time and Worry Jar exercises

Setting aside a dedicated 'Worry Time' to talk with your child about their thoughts and worries can be a very effective strategy. It helps them learn to postpone and interrupt worrying thoughts, and it frees up their minds so that they are able to get on and have a good day. It also helps with worry at bedtime and problems with getting to sleep.[52]

Another useful approach is to help your child or teenager write down their worries on small pieces of paper and put them into a 'Worry Jar' or similar container. This allows them to identify their feelings and let them go. You can then read the worries together a few weeks later and talk about which ones have come to pass and which are still valid. They can rip up and throw away any worries that are no longer pertinent.

Thought diaries

Thought diaries are a helpful way to capture and challenge automatic negative thoughts. Younger children will need some help to complete a thought diary, and it is best to do this at a point in the day when you are able to sit down and spend time together.

It can be similarly helpful for teenagers to use a mood diary to record thoughts and emotions at times when they are feeling anxious or low. Writing things down can provide the starting point for a conversation with you, and it can help them to find perspective by examining their thoughts and considering the extent to which they are realistic. You may decide to agree a time to get together to talk about what they have written down.

Mental health apps

There are many mental health apps available for young people. A fantastic selection to help children and teenagers manage their wellbeing and cope with anxiety or low mood has been compiled on the website for NHS Children and Adolescent Mental Health Services (CAMHS). These include Headspace for meditation, MoodGym, Mind Shift, Calm, No OCD, HappiMe, SAM, Feeling Good Teens, and Worry Tree.[53]

---

52 Meltzer, L.J. & Crabtree, V.M. (2015) *Pediatric Sleep Problems: A Clinician's Guide to Behavioral Interventions.* Washington, DC: APA Books.
53 CAMHS Resources: *Apps.* Available at: https://www.camhs-resources.co.uk/apps-1

Journaling

There are various journals that children can use to help them to express their thoughts and feelings, and to develop self-esteem and emotional resilience. In 2021 The Independent published an excellent list of its fifteen best kids' journals to draw in and write down their feelings.[54]

Positive self-talk and compassion

As we learn about negative thinking and self-criticism, we realise how these can perpetuate anxiety and low mood. For example, when we tell ourselves that we are not as good as other people, or that we are weak, useless or a failure, this is psychologically self-defeating. Our brains tend to recall negative thoughts over positive ones, and so the misery continues.[55]

However, if we choose a compassionate approach towards ourselves, we can learn to train our minds to counter negative self-evaluations by developing alternative positive self-talk. This is the path to increased confidence and self-worth. We can cultivate new and more positive ways of relating to ourselves by reframing negative thoughts and finding positive affirmations, such as "I do have good qualities and strengths. I can try again. It's OK to ask for help." This practice helps us to develop a more positive self-concept, and as such it can be a self-fulfilling and uplifting coping strategy.[56]

---

54 Barton, J. (2021) *15 best kids' journals to draw in and write down their feelings.* Available at: https://www.independent.co.uk/extras/indybest/kids/books/best-kids-journal-child-gratitude-happy-b1821016.html

55 Jantz, G.L. (2016) *The Power of Positive Self-Talk.* Available at: https://www.psychologytoday.com/us/blog/hope-relationships/201605/the-power-positive-self-talk

56 Mead, E. (2021) *What is Positive Self-Talk?* Available at: https://positivepsychology.com/positive-self-talk/

Chapter 11: Recognising avoidant behaviours

Anxious children will often stay away from anything that might trigger their anxiety, which to some extent seems logical enough. However, this method of coping is both unhelpful and ineffective because it provides only short-term relief. In the longer term, it will actually serve to prolong the anxiety. By constantly avoiding potentially stressful situations, the young person never has the opportunity to test their predictions about how bad these situations will really be, and whether they will or will not cope. It is important to help anxious or depressed children to reduce avoidance.

> ## Key Point
> By avoiding stressful situations, a young person never has the opportunity to test their predictions about how bad these situations will really be.

Research evidence suggests that gradual behavioural exposure to feared situations is a key element in the treatment of anxiety disorders in children and young people.[57] This process is called exposure and response prevention, and the assistance of a mental health professional may be required. The purpose of gradual exposure is to help the child to manage and tolerate anxiety as best they can. It gradually enables them to gain more belief in their ability to cope, and it increases confidence and resilience. See the Appendix for a link to accessible, step-by-step guidance for parents.

It takes time to bring about change in avoidant behaviours, so a very gradual approach and exposure to feared situations is required, together with patience and perseverance. Explain to the child or teenager that they may feel anxious, but the level of anxiety will begin to decrease the more often they face the fears. This is known as the 'habituation curve'.[58]

As you begin to work on gradual exposure, it is helpful to agree on some goals and to create a hierarchy of challenges. These can be rated on a ladder, with what the child or young person feels will be easiest to face

---

[57] Plaisted, H., Waite, P., Gordon, K. & Creswell, C. (2021) Optimising Exposure for Children and Adolescents with Anxiety, OCD and PTSD: A Systematic Review. *Clinical child and family psychology review* 24 (2), 348–369.
[58] Child Mind Institute (2020) *What to Do (and Not Do) When Children Are Anxious.* Available at: https://childmind.org/article/what-to-do-and-not-do-when-children-are-anxious/

at the bottom and the most difficult goals at the top. Start small, with the easiest step that they feel they can tackle. Help them to explore coping strategies and identify the ones that they find most effective. Practise these when they are not experiencing a state of anxiety, so that they are able to call upon them when taking each brave step. Help them to repeat each step on the ladder until they feel ready to move onto the next challenge. Small gains can improve their willingness to move forward, and their confidence in themselves to approach the next stage.

It can be very hard not to feel overprotective of an anxious child as they face the situations that cause them distress. However, if we try to help out and allow them to avoid their fears, this can limit their experience and independence, hampering their development of a sense of self-efficacy and their ability to cope with stress or worry. It is often a difficult balance to strike. Encourage the child to have a go at new activities or tasks with the clear message that if things don't work out well the first time, they can try again. You can also help them to develop their confidence by guiding them in problem-solving, rather than simply offering ready-made solutions.

If the child gets stuck and cannot face the situations that you have agreed to approach, the process can be broken into smaller, more manageable steps. If they are unable to move forward at a particular point, it is vital not to force the situation or to show frustration. Praise the young person for attempting or achieving small steps, and emphasise that they can try again when they are ready. Recognise their bravery and strengths. If they face their worries gradually with support, this can help them to develop resilience.

How to help – overcoming avoidant behaviours

☞ Help the child to tolerate and manage their anxiety, and explain that it is not a question of eliminating it. Teach them to be brave by showing them that you believe they can face their fears and encouraging them to try even if they feel scared or worried.

☞ It might be helpful to remind them of a time when they were courageous and overcame something challenging. You can also model healthy ways of handling your own anxiety.

☞ Acknowledge their fears. However, try not to be overprotective and do not enable their avoidance; this just keeps the anxiety going. Avoid asking leading questions or showing that you are worried, as this can reinforce the fear.

☞ Break larger goals into small steps that the child can achieve, and praise their success. Offer positive encouragement that it will be OK. They will manage, but they need to be patient. Help them to see that by worrying less, they can do more and feel better about themselves.

☞ Progress could be rewarded with inexpensive items such as fun stationery, stickers, football cards, treats or special privileges.

☞ Reduce anticipatory anxiety time ahead of a task, and keep the child busy. Think things through together and plan ahead to lessen worries.

☞ Help the child to learn coping skills such as breathing exercises to soothe their anxiety. It is useful to practice these at a time when they are not anxious or low, so that they are equipped in times of need.

☞ A very helpful strategy to instil confidence is for the child to imagine themselves coping well in a scary situation. You can do this together in a fun way before they take their first steps.

☞ Learning positive self-talk can also be a highly beneficial approach. For example, instead of the young person saying to themselves, "I can't do this," encourage them to say instead, "I'll give it a go."

Chapter 12: The school culture and environment

As we saw in Chapter 3, secure attachments are vitally important for the healthy psychological development of our children and young people. Within the educational context, a consistent and supportive relationship between teachers and their pupils is thought to be a key factor in helping young people to feel secure and engage well in the learning process. The Learning Triangle model developed by Heather Geddes emphasises the importance of the attachment relationship between the pupil, their teachers and the learning tasks. Geddes proposes that attachment theory should be the basis for understanding and supporting pupils who are experiencing emotional difficulties. She recommends that this is central to approaches to teacher training and pupil wellbeing in primary education.[60]

> ### Expert View
> *"Contained anxiety can facilitate thinking and learning. Excessive uncertainty can inhibit thinking and learning."*
>
> Heather Geddes[59]

Knowledge of attachment theory in the school environment could help teachers to understand unusual or concerning behaviours, and reduce the risk of misinterpreting insecure, anxious or depressed presentations as disruptive or defiant. In a recent article, Professor Elizabeth Harlow discusses the benefits of adopting the principles of attachment theory in the educational context, both in the teacher-pupil relationship and within the school as a whole. Noting that positive results can be achieved when school leaders encourage a warm socio-emotional climate and a culture of respect, she argues that teachers should be educated in child development and have time to cultivate supportive relationships, but they also need to be authentic, have high expectations of pupils and facilitate pupil autonomy.[61]

---

[59] Geddes, H. (2018). *Attachment, Behaviour and Learning.* Therapy Route. Available at: https://www.therapyroute.com/article/attachment-behaviour-and-learning-by-h-geddes

[60] Geddes, H. (2006) *Attachment in the classroom: The links between children's early experience, emotional well-being, and performance in school.* Worth Publishing.

[61] Headteacher Update (2018) *Attachment Theory in Schools.* Available at: https://www.headteacher-update.com/best-practice-article/attachment-theory-in-schools/167068/

There are also specialist mental health organisations within the UK which offer information and guidance to help educational professionals to implement a whole-school approach to mental health and wellbeing. This involves commitment and collaboration between senior educators, teachers, school staff, parents, carers and the wider community.[62]

A survey of young people's views on happiness and wellbeing conducted by the Office for National Statistics (ONS) in October 2020 highlighted the importance of a supportive school environment to help individuals who are struggling with their mental health. Key areas that young people identified were the school environment and culture, attitudes of staff, the learning curriculum and extra-curricular activities. The things that worried them most included academic pressure and the number of exams they had to take. Of great importance was having somewhere quiet to retreat to in times of stress. This would provide an opportunity to rebalance, relax, and feel safe and calm. Feeling happy was very much dependent on feeling accepted and not judged by others, and this was vital to the young people. They felt that the provision of a safe space that was separate from bullying or critical peers really helped them to cope with these pressures.[26]

Taking such findings into consideration when implementing appropriate support in educational settings is surely the way forward. In my experience, many schools already have pastoral provision in these areas and continually strive to make improvements for the children and young people under their care. In 2018, the Mental Health Foundation launched a campaign in Scotland called Make it Count, which involved embedding whole-school approaches and a focus on the prevention of mental health disorders to ensure healthy, nurturing environments. It is calling on the Government and schools to address all these elements to deliver effective change.

---

62 Anna Freud National Centre for Children and Families: *Whole-school approach*. Available at: https://www.mentallyhealthyschools.org.uk/whole-school-approach

The top five requirements are as follows:

1. All teachers to be trained in mental health and adolescent brain development.
2. All pupils to take part in a 'wellbeing questionnaire' once a term to identify and address problems early.
3. A new national target of one hour of quality Personal and Social Education (PSE) per week with half of those classes dedicated to building emotional resilience.
4. Every school to adopt a peer-led mental health programme to help young people to support one another and tackle stigma.
5. Mental health support workers, in addition to counsellors, to be embedded in every school to provide fast, effective support.[63]

---

63 Mental Health Foundation: *Mental health in schools: Make it Count.* Available at: https://www.mentalhealth.org.uk/campaigns/mental-health-schools-make-it-count-scotland

How to help – supporting children and young people in school

There are many ways in which schools can help young people who may be experiencing anxiety and depression.[64]

- Be vigilant and notice if a pupil seems to be struggling. It is important to be aware that this will be less apparent if the young person internalises their difficulties and/or is quiet and well behaved in class.

- Ask to speak to the pupil in private. Explain that you have noticed that they seem unhappy and ask if they are having a difficult time. Be clear that school is a place where they can be listened to and supported, and that they do not need to be afraid to reach out.

- If a pupil appears to be having a panic attack, direct or accompany them to the designated quiet room in school and contact a mental health colleague. The pupil could bring a friend if they feel it is helpful. For more advice on first aid in times of panic see Chapter 5.

- Encourage the pupil to talk to someone. This could be you, pastoral or mental health staff, their parents or another trusted person. Try to get a sense of whether they are experiencing anxiety or low mood, and if it is related to school or home.

- If the problem is school-related and the pupil is anxious about completing their work, help them to set achievable, realistic goals. Common worries can be around getting things wrong, taking tests and speaking in front of others. Show understanding, think about helpful support strategies for the classroom setting and make adjustments where possible. It is important that any measures put in place are discreet and do not attract the attention of other pupils.

---

64 Adapted from Response Ability: *Social and Emotional Wellbeing: A Teacher's Guide.* Available at: https://s3-ap-southeast-2.amazonaws.com/himh/assets/Uploads/responseability-teachers-guide.pdf

- ☞ Encourage the pupil to be brave and face stressful situations in class. Talk to them about how they could approach this, and agree small, gradual steps that they feel they can manage. Notice and praise each achievement to increase their confidence to continue.

- ☞ Have realistic expectations, be patient, and don't push the young person too hard or overwhelm them. As they become more confident, offer new challenges. For example they could be given some responsibilities at school to promote their self-efficacy, confidence and independence.

- ☞ Talk to the pupil about self-help coping strategies that they could try for their anxiety or low mood. Having a range of websites and resources that you can direct them to can be hugely beneficial. These offer a starting point to help the young person understand what they are going through. They can then either make use of the coping strategies or seek professional support.

- ☞ Younger children may not be able to voice how they feel. In these cases it is advisable to raise your concerns with the school counsellor or designated pastoral or mental health staff. You may also wish to contact the parents if you consider it appropriate. The same factors apply if you are concerned about an older pupil who is not engaging with you and may not be inclined to reach out for support.

- ☞ If the school has a wellbeing programme, encourage the pupil to participate so they can learn about emotions, relaxation and coping strategies. The programme would ideally include groups of several pupils to normalise learning emotional regulation skills. Explain that many children and young people experience similar difficulties, and it is healthy to practise ways to maintain our emotional wellbeing.

- ☞ Check in with the pupil regularly to find out how they are feeling, what progress is being made, and whether additional support is needed.

Chapter 13: In the classroom

It may not be obvious that a pupil is struggling with anxiety or low mood if they internalise their difficulties and are well-behaved in the classroom. To mitigate the risk of overlooking young people who may be struggling, there are considerations that educational staff can bear in mind – and strategies that can be used to support a young person who may be in need of help. A good place to begin is with classroom layout. Anxious children tend to worry about getting into trouble, and can therefore benefit from being seated close to the teacher and away from disruptive pupils. This can enable them to focus better on their schoolwork without stressful distractions.

> ## Key Point
> *It may not be obvious that a pupil is struggling with anxiety or low mood if they internalise their difficulties and are well-behaved in the classroom.*

Young people can often worry about getting things wrong in class, especially when asked to complete a task. Clear, explicit instructions really help, for example writing the task on the board and clearly indicating when it is time to begin and end. Answering questions in front of their classmates can be a source of great anxiety, with pupils being fearful of drawing attention to themselves or of being judged by their peers if they answer a question incorrectly. It can be helpful to have a chat with the young person and offer encouragement, perhaps agreeing that they will start by trying to answer questions to which they definitely know the correct answer. You can then build on this to increase confidence and resilience.

Giving presentations and taking tests

Socially anxious children or teenagers may find giving presentations in front of the class excruciating or too daunting altogether. One way to help them to build confidence could be to allow them to make a video or audio recording at home, and to present it just to the teacher. This can be repeated until the young person feels able to do a very short presentation to a small group, and ultimately to the whole class. This should be a gradual process, undertaken at a pace that is comfortable for the pupil. If a young person is anxious about tests, allowing them extra time can be a great help to alleviate pressure and let them settle into the task. It can also be helpful, where possible, to provide a quiet room without distractions.

Break times

Socially anxious children can be supported by organising each class into small groups that spend breaks and lunchtimes together. This can help the child to feel more content and reduce anticipatory anxiety about who they might spend those times with or whether they will be alone. Alternating between different groups may help to foster friendships and increase social skills and connections with more of their peers. For teenagers this may be harder to achieve, however, and may not be as appropriate or well received.

Managing change

Anxious children and young people often struggle with change and uncertainty. Unfamiliar situations can feel worrying and uncomfortable, and unpredictability and a lack of consistency can trigger anxiety and even panic. A calm, orderly environment is therefore important to help these young people thrive. They cope and perform best when they know what to expect, and when they have a sense that they will be supported if issues arise. Ideally, the classroom should be well-organised and the structure to the day should be clear and predictable. They would benefit from a teacher who is approachable and nurturing, but also clear about what behaviour is acceptable with a calm, firm and non-punitive approach to discipline.

Anxious children are usually 'people pleasers' and want to be able to do what is required of them. When faced with unexpected changes in school routine or teaching staff, the young person may worry that things will go badly because they are unprepared, uncertain and do not feel in control. A good way to deal with this would be to anticipate any upcoming changes and inform the child's parents in advance. This would give them time to talk it over at home and prepare the child to cope when the situation arises.

Go-to person and designated quiet place

Children and young people benefit from having a designated adult who they can go to at school if they are feeling anxious or low. When an understanding person is aware of their difficulties, school can feel like a safe and supportive place where there is someone they trust to speak to if needed. It could be their class teacher, pastoral or mental health staff, a school counsellor or a school nurse. With this support in place, the young person may be more likely to attend school rather than avoiding it, meaning that they will not miss out on schoolwork and the social benefits.

If the go-to person is not available when support is needed, a contingency could be to have a quiet room in school to which the young person can retreat. This allows them space and time to feel calmer and go back into class when they feel ready. Comfortable chairs and soft lighting in this room can create a calm and peaceful space to practice coping strategies.

'Time out' cards

If an anxious young person is feeling out of control, 'time out' cards are a useful tool to signal to a teacher that they need to have some private time to calm down. This allows them to leave the class discreetly without drawing attention to themselves. It is important to agree with the young person that you will trust them to only use the card if really necessary. If a card feels too obvious, alternative ways of signalling can be explored.

Absence from school

If a young person has been absent from school, they can have significant worries about catching up on missed work. A good strategy to allay fears and allow them to get back up to speed is to ask a willing and responsible classmate to help by sharing notes and materials. If the child has missed a class test or one is scheduled on the day they return, show understanding and explain that you can rearrange it for when they have settled back in.

School outings and residential trips

Day trips and residential visits can trigger anxiety about separation from parents, changes to normal routines, or being with a social group in which the young person does not feel comfortable. It can be helpful if the teacher responsible thinks in advance about what might be problematic and puts strategies in place to support the anxious pupil. For example, they could let the pupil know that they will be in the teacher's own group on a class outing or invite parents to attend. Ahead of a residential trip, the school could work with the child's parents and plan short separations, such as sleepovers with friends or family, to prepare them for time away from home.

How to help – in the classroom

☞ Sit anxious pupils close to the teachers and away from disruptive pupils to minimise distractions and allow them to focus.

☞ Provide clear, explicit instructions for tasks – e.g. write the task on the board and indicate clearly when it's time to begin and end.

☞ If a pupil is reluctant to speak in class, offer encouragement and support strategies to build confidence and resilience.

☞ Allow anxious pupils to give presentations in private, or to make a video or audio recording, as a starting point for building skills.

☞ Allow extra time and a quiet room without distractions for pupils who are anxious about taking tests.

☞ Support socially anxious children by organising each class into small groups that spend breaktimes and lunchtimes together.

☞ Provide a calm, predictable environment to support children who worry about uncertainty. Inform parents of any upcoming changes.

☞ Have a designated person that pupils can go to if they are feeling worried or low, and a quiet room to which anxious pupils can retreat.

☞ Use 'time out' cards to allow anxious children to signal that they are feeling out of control and need private time to calm down.

☞ If a pupil is returning after an absence, postpone tests and ask a classmate to help them get back up to speed by sharing notes.

☞ Consider and plan day trips and residential trips carefully in advance so as not to trigger anxiety about separation from parents, changes to normal routines, or being in an unfamiliar social group.

Part 3: Common anxiety problems in children and young people

Chapter 14: Types of anxiety and when to seek help

Anxiety is one of the most prevalent types of mental health difficulty experienced by children and adolescents. It can impact negatively on an individual's confidence, self-worth, academic performance, relationships and quality of life. However, it is important to understand that a certain amount of anxiety is normal for all human beings. Children will have fears and worries just like adults, and it is very natural to feel anxious in stressful situations. It is only when anxiety levels become high and enduring that it can have a negative impact on how we feel and function day-to-day. If our worries prevent us from achieving our goals and doing the things which keep us balanced and happy, it is important to seek support.[65]

> **Key Point**
>
> *If our worries prevent us from achieving our goals and doing the things which keep us balanced and happy, it is important to seek support.*

There are many strategies and therapeutic interventions available to help anxious children and young people to reduce their distress, learn to cope, and maintain their happiness and wellbeing. If anxiety is detected early, they have an excellent chance of recovery. Helping young people to talk about their worries and learn coping strategies can enable them to manage their thoughts, emotions and symptoms. And, by understanding how to recognise anxious behaviours and emotions, we can begin to feel better informed and more confident to intervene before the difficulty reaches a clinical level.

Types of anxiety

There are various types of anxiety which children and young people may experience for different reasons. They include:

- **Generalised anxiety (GAD):** Worries about many different areas of life, such as issues with school, family difficulties or world events.
- **Panic attacks:** Sudden surges of fear and anxiety with distressing and overwhelming bodily symptoms. These can be a feature of all types of anxiety.

---

65 YoungMinds: *Supporting your child with anxiety: A guide for parents.* Available at: https://youngminds.org.uk/find-help/for-parents/parents-guide-to-support-a-z/parents-guide-to-support-anxiety/

- **Panic attacks with agoraphobia:** Fear of having panic attacks in public and unfamiliar places and being unable to escape or get help.
- **Separation anxiety:** Worries about bad things happening when you are away from loved ones.
- **Social anxiety:** Worries based around the belief that others are judging you and thinking of you in negative ways.
- **Obsessive-compulsive anxiety (OCD):** Engagement in and repetition of specific actions, rituals or thoughts to reduce worries and avoid bad things happening.
- **Post-traumatic stress (PTSD):** High levels of anxiety and distressing symptoms following a frightening or traumatic event.[66]

General features and symptoms

Central to all forms of anxiety are thoughts and feelings of uncertainty and threat. The condition is characterised by fears and worries – in particular, 'what if?' concerns and predictions that something bad is going to happen. This can be compounded by the anxious person overestimating the threat and believing that they will be unable to cope if such things come to pass.

When an individual feels anxious, fears about the possibility of bad things happening can be distressing and disproportionate to reality (disconnected from reality). Bodily symptoms can be extreme and long-lasting, and the person can feel out of control. As a result, some people will go to great lengths to avoid anything which triggers their anxiety. Humans are naturally sensitive to change, new situations and things that have felt threatening in the past. We are also receptive to, and can be influenced by, other people's reactions and the ways in which they cope with anxiety.

Anxiety often involves significant physical symptoms. These can be alarming and exhausting, particularly if we try to hide them and cope alone. If we are not aware that such reactions are common, we may feel that there is something wrong with us, that we are not normal or that we are in danger. Misinterpreting bodily symptoms or focusing on them excessively can escalate the anxiety, producing stress hormones such as cortisol and adrenalin. This can result in severe episodes of anxiety and panic attacks.

An anxious young person's worries can have a substantial impact on their happiness, quality of life and daily functioning. They will often avoid situations that provoke their anxiety because they underestimate their ability to cope. This can mean that they miss out on doing things that they would normally enjoy, and it may lead to them feeling unable to go

---

66 NHS inform: *Anxiety disorders in children*. Available at: https://www.nhsinform.scot/illnesses-and-conditions/mental-health/anxiety-disorders-in-children/

to school or socialise. Unfortunately, such avoidance can maintain the anxiety. It can interfere significantly with their enjoyment of life and limit their opportunities and experience. If the anxiety continues untreated, it can lead to low mood or clinical depression.

Various psychological theories and models are used to describe, explain and treat anxiety. Cognitive Behavioural Therapy (CBT) models will be used here to help us understand the nature of the condition and what the individual may be experiencing.[67,68] CBT formulations are useful because they are very accessible for young people and their parents. They help to identify what triggers the anxiety and to illustrate the link between unhelpful thoughts, emotions, physical symptoms and the behaviours that maintain anxiety, as seen in the table below. It is useful to be aware of these different aspects, and to monitor for them if you suspect that your child or teenager may be suffering with anxiety.

Anxious thoughts/cognitions	Anxious emotions
■ Mind racing with fearful predictions, 'what if?' thoughts, anticipation that the worst is going to happen. ■ Catastrophising: "I will not be able to cope when bad things happen." ■ Comparing and despairing: "Others cope well; I'm different and weak." ■ "I'm going mad." ■ "I'm mentally ill and won't get better." ■ "I'll faint, or collapse or go crazy." ■ "I'll make a fool of myself in front of everyone." ■ "People will notice I'm nervous." ■ "There is something wrong with my heart or lungs and I could have a heart attack or stop breathing". ■ "I need to avoid these situations to stay safe and feel under control." ■ "I need to escape to a safe place."	■ Intensely worried most of the time ■ Feeling under threat; hyperalert to anxiety-provoking situations ■ Apprehensive ■ Frightened ■ Panicky ■ Tense, on edge ■ Unsettled, jumpy, restless ■ Unable to relax ■ Unable to concentrate ■ Feeling out of control ■ Exhausted ■ Drained

---

67 Beck, A.T. (1997) The past and future of cognitive therapy. *Journal of Psychotherapy Practice & Research* 6 (4), 276–284.
68 Hofmann, S.G., Asnaani, A., Vonk, I.J., Sawyer, A.T. & Fang, A. (2012) The Efficacy of Cognitive Behavioral Therapy: A Review of Meta-analyses. *Cognitive therapy and research* 36 (5), 427–440.

Physical symptoms of anxiety	Anxious behaviours
■ Difficulty breathing, hyperventilation or shallow breathing ■ Heart pounding, racing or skipping a beat ■ Sensation of tightness or pain in the chest area ■ Dizzy, lightheaded or faint ■ Flushed, feeling hot, sweating (not due to heat), sweaty palms ■ Unsteadiness in legs, hands trembling ■ Sensation of choking ■ Dry mouth ■ Indigestion or stomach ache ■ Butterflies, nausea, stomach churning ■ Appetite disturbance ■ Urges to go to the toilet; bladder urgency or diarrhoea ■ Muscle tension; body aches ■ Numbness or tingling in the toes or fingers, cold hands ■ Difficulty getting to sleep, waking in the night and inability to fall asleep again	■ Unexplained crying or sadness ■ Avoiding anything which causes worry or uncertainty ■ Seeking reassurance ■ Being clingy and not wanting to be away from safe place (e.g. home and parents) ■ Resisting going to new places or meeting new people ■ Social withdrawal, being quieter in social gatherings, not talking or interacting ■ Shyness, self-consciousness and sensitivity to criticism ■ Spending long periods alone worrying and ruminating ■ Uncharacteristic irritability and frustrated behaviour ■ Losing temper easily ■ Restlessness, inability to relax or sit still ■ Procrastination and over-preparation, taking a long time to complete tasks and worrying that they aren't good enough ■ Deterioration in academic performance due to inability to concentrate ■ School avoidance or refusal ■ Biting fingernails, picking skin, pulling hair ■ Over- or under-eating

The fight-or-flight response

The physical symptoms of anxiety are best understood in terms of the response of the primitive human brain to any kind of threat: fight-or-flight (sometimes expanded to fight, flight or freeze). Our caveman ancestors needed to be constantly alert to protect themselves from deadly attacks by predators. Their brains had an inbuilt survival mechanism which enabled them to be vigilant to any threat, and either fight or escape from danger.

> **Key Point**
>
> When the amygdala is activated, the body is swiftly charged with stress hormones to ensure our ability to fight or flee from the danger.

Today, our bodies react in just the same way. When the part of the brain that detects threat (the *amygdala*) is activated, the body is swiftly charged with stress hormones to ensure our ability to fight or flee from the danger, whether real or perceived. Adrenaline and cortisol cause our blood sugar, blood pressure and pulse rate to increase, our breathing to become more rapid, our muscles to tense and our pupils to dilate. Our heart rate increases, rapidly sending blood to where it is needed most. All this happens instantly and automatically. It primes our bodies to be faster, stronger and more alert, enabling us to defend ourselves or escape. Once the threat has passed, our bodies naturally release different hormones to help our muscles relax.

The fight-or-flight reaction becomes a problem, however, when this kind of action is initiated in response to things that are not actually life-threatening. Anxious people are on constant high alert against threat, and if danger is incorrectly perceived, the brain's internal alarm system is falsely triggered and the body reacts instinctively, without higher level thought processes. This can impact physical wellbeing and contribute to stress and mental health problems.[69] Recognising the thoughts that trigger anxiety and govern how the body reacts is an important step in anxiety management. We can then learn to challenge unrealistic and catastrophic thoughts, and adopt coping strategies to calm and soothe our sympathetic nervous system.[70]

The fight-or-flight response is also believed to play a significant role in panic attacks. An important part of the process of treating and recovering from anxiety is to realise that the worst did not happen after all, and that the physical symptoms of anxiety naturally rise and fall without causing serious damage to our health.

---

69 Harvard Health Publishing: *Understanding the stress response*. Available at: https://www.health.harvard.edu/staying-healthy/understanding-the-stress-response
70 New York Times (2016) *Outsmarting Our Primitive Responses to Fear*. Available at: https://www.nytimes.com/2017/10/26/well/live/fear-anxiety-therapy.html

How to help – when to seek professional support

 Parents and carers will understandably feel concerned about the emotional wellbeing of a child or teenager if they are displaying uncharacteristic moods or behaviours. Sometimes the young person may simply be going through a temporary difficult period, which is quite natural. It can be difficult to know when we need more support. Some of the reasons to reach out for professional help are as follows:

- Anxiety and/or low mood is frequently preventing the child from enjoying home or school life, affecting their usual daily functioning and having a significant negative impact on their emotional wellbeing.
- Anxiety levels are high and long lasting, and self-help has not been effective in relieving the distress.
- The young person's worries are out of proportion and unrealistic.
- The symptoms of anxiety are frequent and intense, appear out of control and lead to panic attacks.
- The young person's avoidance of situations is significant, and they are unable to do things that they used to enjoy.

 If you feel that professional support is required, possible sources of help and referral include:

- School counsellor or psychologist
- GP referral to NHS Children and Young People Mental Health Services
- Community youth counselling organisations
- Private mental health organisations

 Links to further information and resources can be found in the Appendix.

Chapter 15: Generalised anxiety

Although all young people naturally experience fears and worries as they grow up, some have longer-term problems with anxiety. Children with Generalised Anxiety Disorder (GAD) can feel anxious every day and worry about many areas of their lives. They often find it very difficult to feel relaxed and content. If the individual does not receive support or treatment, this can continue into the teenage years and adulthood. While specific approaches to each type of anxiety are given in the relevant chapters of this book, much of the information and advice contained in this chapter on generalised anxiety is applicable to all types of anxiety. While the nature of the fears may vary, the general themes and strategies will be similar.

> **Key Point**
>
> *Children with Generalised Anxiety Disorder (GAD) can feel anxious every day and worry about many areas of their lives.*

General features and symptoms

For young people with GAD, the overarching worry commonly involves a persistent and exaggerated fear that something bad is going to happen. They perceive that they will be unable to manage many aspects of their lives, becoming preoccupied with unrealistic worries about a wide variety of things that could go wrong in everyday experiences. In other words, the threat of these things coming to pass is overestimated, and the young person also underestimates their ability to cope.

Parents and teachers may have some awareness that these young people are 'born worriers' who have always shown anxious tendencies. A great deal of reassurance is often needed about the many things that concern them. This could be around completing schoolwork, making mistakes, or losing the approval or support of important people in their lives. Such ongoing and excessive preoccupation may understandably be distressing and difficult for young people to manage. Unless they have support, they can feel alone in their thoughts. If these worries are internalised and not shared with significant and trusted people, the suffering continues.

Generalised anxiety can involve elements of many different types of worry, such as separation anxiety or social anxiety. Anxious children and young people often do not cope well with change and uncertainty. It is important to be aware of the trigger factors, and to help them to tolerate change and associated worries. A range of useful workbooks is available on the subject.[71]

The key features of GAD include:

- Fear of change and unpredictability. Difficulty in tolerating and coping with uncertainty.
- Excessive, unrealistic fears about many day-to-day occurrences.
- Difficulties in controlling worry about multiple situations such as academic performance, human tragedy and health-related issues.
- Difficulty concentrating; always thinking about what's happening next.
- 'What if?' concerns that reach far into the future.
- Rumination and an over developed sense of responsibility: a belief that worrying helps us to predict and protect against bad things happening, and that tragedies are preventable by worry.
- Fear that any negative thing that happens to others could also happen to you.
- Social anxieties including excessive worries about making mistakes or failure; fear of loss of approval, criticism or negative evaluation from others regarding personal qualities, abilities and academic performance.
- Reviewing events to make sure you didn't hurt anyone's feelings or do anything wrong.
- Self-esteem levels being largely dependent on maintaining positive relationships and the approval of others.
- Low risk-taking; need for reassurance and approval of small steps.
- Physical symptoms of anxiety, low mood, irritability, sleep difficulties and fatigue.

---

71 Plummer, D., Harper, A. & ProQuest (Firm) (2010) *Helping children to cope with change, stress, and anxiety: A photocopiable activities book.* London: Jessica Kingsley Publishers.

Generalised anxiety disorder (GAD) case study: Niamh, age 8

Niamh was a bright, loving and kind-natured child. She had been prone to worry from around the age of five. Her parents were concerned that she was suffering with a range of anxieties that had persisted for more than a year. Niamh seemed to be constantly worrying 'what if?' various bad things would happen, engaging in a multitude of thoughts and questions and trying to predict every possible scenario ahead of time. She was troubled about things that realistically might never happen, and she was spending long periods in distress and rumination.

Due to the intensity and duration of Niamh's anxiety, her parents felt overwhelmed and at a loss as to how best to support their daughter. They had sought a referral for Cognitive Behavioural Therapy (CBT), recognising the importance of intervening as soon as possible to help Niamh to manage her anxiety, worry less and develop better coping skills – and, of course, to improve her emotional wellbeing, self-confidence and resilience.

Approximately a year earlier, Niamh's mother had needed to go into hospital for a minor procedure, and her parents suspected that this had been a significant contributing factor to Niamh's anxiety. A range of other influences also seemed to frequently trigger her anxious feelings. These included viewing films that were not age-appropriate and witnessing media reports of natural disasters, human tragedy and suffering. Niamh was overrun with fearful predictions and catastrophic thoughts about such harm befalling herself, her loved ones or people in general. She began to experience separation issues, and her unhelpful predictions provoked extreme anxiety and high levels of distress. Niamh also became very worried when bad things such as illness, accidents, getting lost or being burgled happened to her loved ones. She was highly sensitive to making mistakes and losing the approval of others, and preoccupied with needing to ensure that she was liked or loved.

Individual/idiosyncratic formulation: Niamh

Anxious thoughts/cognitions	Anxious emotions
- "If I worry, it could help me to prepare and protect." - Catastrophising: "What if something awful happens to my family or friends? The world isn't a safe place. They could get lost, have an accident, get hurt, get ill or die." - "I am going mad and will be put in a hospital." - "I cannot cope if anything goes wrong." - "I will cry and lose control and it will be awful and unbearable." - "I must keep this to myself and not tell anyone in case these things happen." - Mind-reading: "People know I'm anxious. They'll think I'm mad if I talk about it." - Comparing and despairing: "It's only me that's scared all the time." - Fortune-telling: "If I get things wrong, people will not like me and will stay away from me." - Shoulds and musts: "I must not get anything wrong. I must not upset anyone."	- Excessively and intensely worried most days - Mind racing with 'what if?' questions and thoughts - Feeling unsafe - Apprehensive and afraid - Agitated, tense and easily startled - Unable to relax - Poor concentration - Exhausted - Unhappy and often tearful - Helpless

Physical symptoms of anxiety	Anxious behaviours
■ Irregular breathing; hyperventilation ■ Heart beating fast ■ Dizzy ■ Hot ■ Shaky; hands trembling ■ Butterflies in stomach ■ Poor appetite ■ Poor quality of sleep and difficulty falling asleep	■ Tearful and crying often ■ Ruminating and worrying for long periods ■ Clingy; not wanting to be away from parents ■ Hypervigilant of anything going wrong ■ Frequently seeking reassurance ■ Avoiding watching TV programmes, going on holiday, or going to sleepovers ■ Avoiding talking about her worries and becoming distressed when asked about them ■ Checking everyone is happy and OK ■ Unable to sit down and settle for long ■ Unable to relax and get to sleep at night

What helped Niamh with her GAD?

Adopt and model a calm approach to the situation. Explain to the young person what you know about the problem and how it can feel, and normalise it. Identify the main issues and reasons for their worries.

Niamh attended CBT sessions with her mother. The therapist explained the nature and symptoms of anxiety, and how children with the condition can have worrying thoughts about bad things which never actually come to pass. He normalised Niamh's experiences by telling her that he worked with lots of young people with anxiety, and he explained that although worry is natural in all human beings, sometimes we need help to manage it. This instilled hope in Niamh that she could be helped to feel better and that she wasn't the only person to have so many worries. It was also encouraging to her mother, who thought that the sessions could be helpful for her too.

Cultivate emotional awareness. Help the young person to identify and cope with their emotions. Show understanding and validate their feelings.

Niamh engaged extremely well with the therapist. With the comfort of her mother's presence, she was able to share her feelings. Niamh talked about feeling nervous and afraid, and constantly worrying about everything. She said that she often had to fight back tears because she was so unhappy, and that it seemed like it would never end. The therapist introduced a feelings book that explained what children experience when they are anxious. This was of great help and served to demonstrate to Niamh that the way she was feeling was not strange or unusual. The therapist acknowledged how tough it had been for Niamh to feel this way, and how exhausting and lonely it must have been for her to bottle up her feelings. Niamh often cried while expressing her emotions, and she was met with compassion, understanding and praise for her bravery.

Help the young person to learn and practise self-regulating and soothing coping strategies to manage symptoms. Adopt strategies for general wellbeing.

The emotional and physical symptoms of Niamh's anxiety were addressed by teaching her self-soothing skills such as deep breathing, progressive muscle relaxation and calming visualisations. She was then encouraged to practise these skills at a time when she was not experiencing high levels of anxiety. This enabled her to develop coping strategies ahead of time and employ them effectively when most needed. Niamh's parents were coached in helping her to learn and adopt these approaches. In addition to this, the therapist helped Niamh to recognise the importance of engaging in plenty of physical activity to improve her mood, sleep and general wellbeing.

Help the young person to identify and challenge negative thoughts and worries. Develop alternative, more realistic thoughts and positive self-talk. Speak to them about the link between unhelpful thoughts, emotions and behaviours.

The thoughts of young people with GAD tend to be automatically catastrophic and pessimistic in nature, such as "What's the worst thing that could happen in this situation?". They often believe that worry has a useful function, enabling them to prepare in advance for bad things happening. They may feel that predicting negative events is a useful and protective coping strategy, even if these things never actually come to pass.

The therapist and Niamh's parents helped her to find a safe space to talk about her anxious thoughts. She was encouraged to adopt alternative, more realistic and helpful perspectives, such as "How likely is it that the worst will actually happen?" and "What is the most likely thing you believe will happen in this situation?". Niamh's anxiety was normalised, and she was helped to realise that TV programmes about awful things happening would naturally cause concern for most people. This process helped Niamh to put her anxious thoughts and fearful predictions into perspective and to feel less worried. It is helpful for children to understand how the mind can play unhelpful tricks by catastrophising, racing ahead and bombarding us with warnings. They can then learn how to challenge the voice of worry, turning the volume down on their concerns and up on more helpful, realistic and rational thinking.

The therapist introduced two books to help Niamh understand how worry works.[72,73] Niamh also used a worry diary to record her concerns and assess the accuracy of her beliefs. She and her parents agreed to meet for a fifteen minute 'Worry Time' each day, during which they would discuss what was on her mind. This helped Niamh to spend less time in rumination, to set aside her anxious thoughts until a specific and limited timeframe, and to reduce apologetic and reassurance-seeking behaviours. A similarly effective approach is to write anxious thoughts on pieces of paper and keep them in a Worry Jar until Worry Time. More information on how to manage and conduct these strategies and the rationale/benefits can be found in Chapter 10.

Help the young person to recognise and understand any unhelpful and avoidant behaviours. Talk about helping them to reduce symptoms by gradually facing their fears and trying to get back to enjoying life.

Niamh was a considerate and caring girl who was vulnerable to the loss of love and approval. She was inclined as a result to try to please others and to seek constant reassurance that everyone was OK and happy with her. The therapist encouraged Niamh to trust how loved she was and to reduce reassurance-seeking behaviours, as such behaviours provide only temporary relief from anxiety.

---

72 Huebner, D. & Matthews, B. (2009) *What to Do When You Worry Too Much: A Kid's Guide to Overcoming Anxiety*. Paw Prints.

73 Huebner, D. & McHale, K. (2020) *Something bad happened: A kid's guide to coping with difficult world news*. London: Jessica Kingsley Publishers.

Niamh also tended to apologise frequently for her anxious thoughts and behaviours. Her parents learned to model a calm and matter-of-fact attitude when she expressed her worries. They helped her to bring her fearful thoughts into perspective. It is important to encourage children to identify and express anxious thoughts rather than avoiding sharing them, as this can be a major factor in maintaining anxiety.

Niamh had been avoiding watching TV or films that she used to enjoy for fear that her anxiety would be triggered. She had begun to socialise less and was distressed about not being able to spend time with her friends in case they didn't like her or found her 'weird'. She was encouraged to gradually begin to watch age-appropriate TV and films again, and to discuss any worrying thoughts which arose with her parents and find perspective. She could then gradually begin to spend more time with her friends again.

Outside of sessions with the therapist, Niamh and her parents worked consistently to identify her worries as they arose, challenge their validity, and employ the recommended coping and calming techniques. Happily, the outcome assessment scores were positive, with Niamh reporting new-found confidence in coping with her fears. She had actually been sharing the coping strategies with friends – a triumph indeed in normalising worries for herself and others. Continued practice would be essential to reinforce these skills and build Niamh's resilience and self-efficacy in coping with her anxieties.

How to help – generalised anxiety

☞ Help the child to learn about the nature of anxiety and its prevalence among children and young people, in order to offer reassurance and normalise their experiences.

☞ Provide a safe space for them to share and identify their feelings. Acknowledge the challenges they face with compassion and understanding.

☞ Help the child to learn self-soothing techniques and to practise these when they are not experiencing high levels of anxiety so that they can be employed effectively in times of need. Encourage other activities that will boost mood and general wellbeing, such as physical exercise.

☞ Help the child to identify unhelpful or pessimistic thoughts, recognise the effect these are having, and bring them into perspective. Help and encourage them to adopt more realistic and helpful thoughts.

☞ Worry diaries, Worry Time or Worry Jar exercises can be a very effective tools for sharing, monitoring and managing concerns.

☞ Work with the child to recognise any unhelpful or avoidant behaviours that they have developed in response to their anxieties. Support them to gradually challenge these habits so that they can enjoy life again.

Chapter 16: Social anxiety

Social anxiety involves feeling high levels of worry and self-consciousness in a variety of social settings. We can all feel uncomfortable at times around other people, or around people we haven't met before, but social anxiety is much more than just being shy. Social interactions with other people can consistently cause feelings of intense discomfort and worry in the socially anxious person. This can impact negatively on an individual's day-to-day functioning and enjoyment of life. Socially anxious young people may also typically avoid talking about their worries. This is a common type of anxiety affecting their age group, however, and it can feel excruciating.

> **Key Point**
>
> *Social anxiety involves feeling high levels of worry and self-consciousness in a variety of social settings.*

While social anxiety can be experienced by younger children, it primarily affects teenagers. It typically occurs in relation to puberty and the accompanying stages of emotional and social development. However, if social anxiety persists for more than six months, and is affecting the young person's wellbeing and functioning, it can develop into a more chronic condition. Early detection and intervention are therefore key to ensuring that a young person receives the understanding and support needed to prevent their social anxiety becoming worse or persisting into adulthood.

General features and symptoms

Social anxiety is characterised by extreme self-consciousness and aversion to being the centre of attention. There is also a great fear of being seen as anxious and being embarrassed or humiliated in almost any social situation. The principal worry is around being judged negatively by others. This can make it very difficult for the person to participate in social activities, and they will often avoid eye contact and talking with or speaking in front of other people.

Social anxiety can interfere with a young person's willingness to attend school, and consequently affect their academic performance. They may have great trouble in forming and maintaining friendships, and will often avoid socialising. It can be a lonely and isolating experience, leading to low mood. Parents and teachers may not recognise social anxiety because a child or teenager is seen as simply shy or of a quiet temperament.

Below are some situations that children and young people with social anxiety may typically avoid because they are anxious about being the focus of attention, feeling embarrassed or being judged negatively by others.

- Being exposed to the observation of others
- Meeting new people and having to speak to them; social events such as family occasions, parties or dates
- Being the focus of attention; speaking in front of the class or in public
- Taking tests or being observed when performing
- Any event where they anticipate a negative response, teasing or criticism from others
- Eating or drinking in view of others
- Speaking on the telephone
- Going to school if there are any issues with peers, friends or teachers

Anxious thoughts/cognitions	Anxious emotions
■ "I won't know what to say to them." ■ "They will probably find me boring." ■ "They will look at me and know I'm anxious and pathetic." ■ "I will get all flustered and go red." ■ "My voice will be shaky." ■ "I will clam up or freeze." ■ "They'll think I'm stupid and weird." ■ "I'll make a fool of myself in front of everyone." ■ "I can't face it." ■ "There's something wrong with me." ■ "Why can't I cope like everyone else?" ■ "They all like socialising; it's just me." ■ "I'll look so stupid." ■ "It will be awful and unbearable." ■ Ruminating afterwards and examining how it went. ■ Focusing on the negative and what did not go well. ■ Viewing oneself in a negative way and being self-critical.	■ Fear and nervous anticipation ■ Dreading having to meet other people and make conversation ■ Tense and on edge ■ Worried ■ Overwhelmed ■ Vulnerable and exposed ■ Self-conscious ■ Humiliated ■ Embarrassed

Physical symptoms of anxiety	Anxious behaviours
■ Face goes red (blushes) ■ Shaky body/hands, trembling ■ Dizzy/lightheaded ■ Blurred vision ■ Shallow breathing, hyperventilation ■ Shaky voice ■ Butterflies/nausea ■ Bodily tension ■ Heart racing/pounding ■ Hot and sweaty	■ Excusing self from social situations (family gatherings, parties, making conversation, speaking in public) ■ Avoiding situations where they have to perform in any way ■ Over-preparing what they might say ■ Engaging in 'safety' behaviours to avoid feeling anxious and being noticed, such as: ▪ leaving as early as possible ▪ staying in the background ▪ trying not to attract attention ▪ speaking quietly or not at all ▪ avoiding eye contact ▪ only spending time with people with whom they are comfortable ▪ only going out with 'safe' people ▪ drinking alcohol for confidence

Social anxiety case study: Marcus, age 14

Marcus's parents described him as a gentle, sensitive and shy boy, especially around teachers and other children. He found change of any kind difficult and did not like to be in busy social environments. He seemed happiest when he was at home with his family. Teaching staff at his primary school were aware of and sensitive to his difficulties.

Marcus transitioned to secondary school with an established group of friends, which his parents felt had helped him to adjust well to the new setting. They noticed, however, that Marcus didn't seem to be making many friends outside his group. They had also become increasingly aware that Marcus was reluctant to go to social events beyond family gatherings, and he had not joined any extracurricular activities at school or in his free time. Due to his quiet temperament, Marcus's parents had understandably not noticed that he was actually experiencing social anxiety. He internalised his worries and tended not to verbalise any problems that he was having.

It had become clear from Marcus's recent behaviour that he was feeling down. His parents were concerned because he was spending a lot of time by himself and hadn't been seeing his friends, who were important to him. When Marcus came out of his room at mealtimes, he was particularly quiet and seemed to be in a low mood. His parents expressed their concerns, but he didn't want to talk about it. He seemed irritated and on edge when asked what was on his mind. Marcus's mother managed to find a quiet moment to speak with him. She said that she would like to be there for him if he wanted to talk about how he was feeling and what was making him so miserable. Marcus listened but declined to talk at the time.

Marcus eventually shared that the trigger for his anxiety had been a new boy joining his friendship group. This boy was ignoring and excluding Marcus. When they did interact, he was offhand and hostile, sometimes giving Marcus dirty looks. This made Marcus feel extremely uncomfortable and distressed, and he began to avoid interacting with the group. It transpired that the other members of the group were not aware of what was happening. Marcus interpreted this as a sign that they didn't care, and he even began to think that they didn't like him any longer. Unfortunately, Marcus's avoidance culminated in him feeling isolated, rejected and extremely low. Sometimes, social anxiety does not become wholly apparent until it is activated by a specific incident of this nature.

Individual/idiosyncratic formulation: Marcus

 Anxious thoughts/cognitions

- "The new boy hates me and will say bad things about me to my friends. They won't like me anymore."
- "Maybe they are tired of me and find me boring."
- "If I try to meet up, they might not want me there."
- "What if they completely ignore me?"
- "I can't face it."
- "They do contact me sometimes, but only because they feel they have to."
- "I can't cope with feeling cast out."
- "They'll see that I'm anxious and think I'm pathetic and weird. It will be unbearable if that happens."
- "If I don't interact with them, it will be a relief."
- "I won't go and that will feel better and safer."
- "I should be able to cope with this."
- "Others cope much better than me and are far more confident."
- "I'm useless and weak."

 Anxious emotions

- Dread and anticipatory anxiety ahead of meeting
- Nervous
- Tense and on edge
- Vulnerable and exposed
- Overwhelmed and distressed
- Embarrassed
- Humiliated
- Hopeless
- Depressed
- Alone

 Physical symptoms of anxiety

- Nausea
- Headaches
- Hyperventilation/shallow breathing
- Heart pounding
- Hot, face goes red (blushing)
- Body/hands shaky, trembling
- Dizzy/lightheaded
- Bodily tension

 Anxious behaviours

- Avoiding contact with friends
- Lack of eye contact or conversation
- Declining any invitations to meet up
- Withdrawing/isolating self
- Socialising much less with safe people/family
- Staying in background and keeping quiet so as not to attract attention
- Avoiding talking about feelings
- Spending time alone ruminating and focusing on the negative

What helped Marcus with his social anxiety?

Adopt and model a calm approach to the situation. Explain to the young person what you know about the problem and how it can feel, and normalise it. Identify the main issues and reasons for their worries.

Marcus's mother spoke with a counsellor about how to support her son, as she felt that his social anxiety might make it difficult for him to work directly with someone he didn't know. Marcus's mum met with the counsellor six times over a period of three months. The counsellor gave Marcus's mother materials such as thought diaries and psychoeducational materials around negative thinking styles. They also talked about how Marcus's anxiety was affecting his mother and ways in which she could maintain her own wellbeing. The counsellor recommended a self-help book for parents containing CBT strategies and evidence-based techniques to use as a framework for helping Marcus.[74]

Cultivate emotional awareness. Help the young person to identify and cope with their emotions. Show understanding and validate their feelings.

Marcus's mother reached out to let him know that she wanted to help and was available to listen when he was ready. They used mood cards to help him identify and talk about his emotions. Marcus was able to explain how he dreaded spending time with his friends in case his thoughts were true that they didn't like him anymore and they preferred the new boy in their group. He was very afraid of feeling unliked, and of the embarrassment and humiliation he would experience if this was the case. It made him feel nervous, tense, sad and alone. Marcus was relieved to share his feelings with his mother, saying that he no longer felt so isolated and that maybe he was misinterpreting the situation. His mother told him that she was always there to talk about his feelings and that she felt honoured that he could confide in her. He acknowledged this with a hug and a smile.

---

74 Willetts, L. & Creswell, C. (2007) *Overcoming your child's shyness and social anxiety: a self-help guide using cognitive behavioral techniques*. London: Constable & Robinson.

Help the young person to learn and practise self-regulating and soothing coping strategies to manage symptoms. Adopt strategies for general wellbeing.

Marcus tried out several self-soothing and coping strategies. His parents also arranged for him to download a phone app that contained many of these practices. He realised that he could feel better if he socialised more because he missed his friends. He also chose to become more active and agreed to go cycling and walking with his parents. He began to think about joining sports activities and clubs. Marcus spent more time with his parents and less time in his room. He joined them more often for family meals, and they ensured that they had the healthy foods that he particularly liked.

Help the young person to identify and challenge negative thoughts and worries. Develop alternative, more realistic thoughts and positive self-talk. Speak to them about the link between unhelpful thoughts, emotions and behaviours.

Due to his social anxiety, Marcus was thinking in the following ways.

- Mind-reading that his friends were thinking negatively about him.
- Making predictions and fortune-telling that his friends had lost interest in him and his friendships were doomed.
- Catastrophising that the worst was going to happen and that it would be unbearable; overestimating the likelihood of these things coming to pass and underestimating his ability to cope.
- Personalising and assuming that his friends were focusing on him.
- Labelling himself, feeling negative and being self-critical.

Marcus's mother listened and helped him to identify and express his negative thoughts. She showed empathy, acknowledging and validating his emotions. She didn't minimise his concerns or judge them from her own frame of reference. Marcus's mother showed that she could understand how these fearful thoughts were making him feel, even though she herself felt that they were exaggerated and probably not realistic. She could appreciate that if these thoughts were facts, Marcus would feel and act in the way he did. She explained the nature of anxiety and that it was natural to feel worried if unpleasant people came into an established group of friends.

Having supported Marcus in identifying his negative thoughts, his mother helped him to examine them, take a step back and put them into perspective. His friends were still contacting him and could be wondering why he was not replying. They may have been totally unaware of what he was experiencing with the new boy in their group. Where was the evidence that they didn't care or want to be with him? How likely was this to be the case? Was there a more balanced and realistic way of looking at things? The evidence was that they had been good and loyal friends since primary school. Marcus was able to acknowledge that his thoughts could be catastrophic, exaggerated and unrealistic. There was no evidence that they were true. His mother helped him to realise that his friends probably didn't realise how he'd been thinking and feeling. If they did notice, they would more than likely be sympathetic and kind. Marcus agreed to speak with the boy he trusted most in his group.

Help the young person to recognise and understand any unhelpful and avoidant behaviours. Talk about helping them to reduce symptoms by gradually facing their fears and trying to get back to enjoying life.

Marcus and his mother made a plan of action together. He agreed to gradually reach out to his friends and become part of the group again, and not to assume the worst. Avoiding them was making him feel miserable, and he realised that he could feel much better if he rejoined them.

In the longer term, Marcus's mother encouraged him to think about expanding his social skills and to consider that it may be good to develop new interests and gain more friends. Joining sporting clubs and being more physically active would be a great way to feel better and improve his general wellbeing. They discussed things he might like to do to approach this, and he planned to take small and manageable steps towards his goals.

How to help – social anxiety

☞ Educate yourself about social anxiety and negative thinking styles so that you are aware of what the child may be experiencing and the most effective ways to help. Share what you have learned with the child and normalise what they are feeling.

☞ If professional support is required but the child's social anxiety would make this difficult, it may be appropriate for parents to seek advice separately and apply this later at home. Resources such as self-help guides and thought diaries can be used as a basis for support.

☞ Let the child know that you want to help and are available to talk when they are ready. Mood cards and other resources can help the child to identify and begin to talk about their feelings. Show empathy, validate their emotions and acknowledge their achievement in sharing their experiences. Reassure them that you will always be there to listen.

☞ Introduce the child to self-soothing and coping strategies and allow them to decide what would work best for them. Encourage them to understand how spending more time with family and friends in positive ways can help them to feel better and less anxious in social situations. This can be achieved in small, manageable steps that build their confidence over time. Help the child to adopt other strategies for general wellbeing, such as becoming more physically active.

☞ Work with the child to examine their negative thoughts and put them into perspective. Help them to challenge these thoughts by looking for evidence of whether they are true and thinking about alternative, more realistic and more helpful interpretations.

☞ Help the child to recognise any avoidant behaviours, and to think about ways to address them. Begin with small, achievable steps and talk about the benefits these will bring. Make plans to improve and maintain the child's general wellbeing to support their progress.

Chapter 17: Panic and agoraphobia

Panic Disorder is a common anxiety problem causing sudden panic attacks that are often recurring. These surges of fear and anxiety tend to arise without warning, and produce bodily symptoms that can feel distressing, overwhelming and out of control. Children and young people are usually more vulnerable to the disorder if they already have anxiety or other mental health difficulties. This can be exacerbated if they are under stress or experiencing a difficult time due to adverse life events such as friendship issues, bereavement or problems at home or in school.

> **Key Point**
>
> Panic Disorder is a common anxiety problem causing sudden panic attacks that can feel distressing, overwhelming and out of control.

Panic Disorder can progress in intensity over time, and early intervention is important to prevent escalation. With timely identification, an approach based on self-help resources and support can be successful. Effective treatments for panic attacks also include mindfulness and CBT.[75]

General features and symptoms

People with Panic Disorder tend to think in a catastrophic way and are extremely fearful of the physical symptoms felt during a panic attack. They often interpret what they are experiencing as dangerous; for example, they may believe that a pounding heart could lead to a heart attack. They can also feel trapped and unable to escape or access help. They may go to great lengths to avoid experiencing or worsening the panic symptoms.

Anxiety levels can be intense during a panic attack, causing people to feel tense, frightened and out of control. It can also lead to general feelings of irritability and hopelessness. Having undergone a serious panic attack, a person may become fearful of experiencing such bodily sensations again. This can cause them to be hypervigilant and constantly scan for signs of an attack, even when they are not in an

---

75 Kim, Y.K. (2019) Panic Disorder: Current Research and Management Approaches. *Psychiatry investigation 16 (1), 1–3.*

anxiety-provoking situation. This excessive focus tends to produce additional adrenalin and cortisol, which can exacerbate the symptoms. The individual may also spend long periods worrying about being in any kind of situation that might cause them anxiety. This can maintain their anxiety and increase the likelihood of them avoiding these situations altogether. The sorts of situations avoided might include:

- Going to places where there will be large numbers of people, such as shopping centres, cinemas, public festivals, or sports stadiums
- Travelling by any type of public transport
- Attending large family or social events, such as weddings or parties.
- Physical exertion, in case it causes symptoms similar to a panic attack, for example shortness of breath or the heart beating faster
- Consuming caffeine or energy drinks that could increase the heart rate
- Venturing out without a trusted and 'safe' person as a companion

Physical symptoms

The physical symptoms of a panic attack can be many and varied, as listed below. However, although the physical symptoms of panic can be incredibly alarming, they are not life-threatening in themselves. A typical attack may last between five and twenty minutes. It can be helpful to compare the anxiety to a wave which rises and then falls away. It is important to remember that the wave will subside, and the body will return to its normal state.

- Heart pounding or tightness in the chest area
- Hyperventilation or shortness of breath
- Nausea and/or stomach pains
- Feeling shaky or trembling
- Feeling light-headed or dizzy
- A sense of dread
- Fear of dying, going mad or losing control
- Numbness, tingling or pins and needles
- Urgency for the toilet
- Sensation of throat closing or choking
- Hot flushes or cold sweats
- Dryness in the mouth
- Derealisation; feeling detached, unreal or in a dream

Due to how severe a panic attack can feel, people sometimes believe that there is something wrong with them, such as a weak heart or lung problems. It is important to have this checked by a GP if you are concerned.

Thoughts

Thoughts in relation to panic attacks are often catastrophic in nature. People can feel convinced that something awful is going to happen. Examples include:

- "There is something wrong with my heart. I could have a heart attack and die."
- "My lungs aren't working properly. I can't breathe. I could suffocate."
- "I am going to be sick."
- "My throat will close, and I will choke and die."
- "If I don't get to the toilet, I will have an accident."
- "I am going to pass out and faint in front of everyone."
- "I cannot go there. No one will help me or get me to hospital."
- "I am going mad. I will lose control and go to pieces."
- "I am mentally ill and will end up in hospital."
- "I will make a total fool of myself in front of everyone. It will be humiliating."

Agoraphobia

Agoraphobia is defined as "an excessive, irrational fear of being in open or unfamiliar places, resulting in the avoidance of public situations from which escape may be difficult".[76] It can involve fear of being in open, crowded, or enclosed spaces and being far from home in remote places. Agoraphobia is classified as a separate condition to panic disorder, and it is not always caused by or related to the fear of having a sudden panic attack in places that feel unsafe. It could be fear of a number of other embarrassing/humiliating situations in which the individual believes they won't be able to escape or get help, such as being physically sick or tripping and falling over in public. Although agoraphobia sometimes occurs on its own without panic disorder, it often develops as a complication of panic disorder whereby there is extreme fear and avoidance of situations for fear of having a panic attack or where a previous attack has happened.[77]

---

76 https://dictionary.apa.org/agoraphobia
77 https://www.nhs.uk/mental-health/conditions/agoraphobia/overview/.

Agoraphobia is not common in young children but adolescents who suffer from panic attacks can often develop the condition. If a panic attack has already taken place in a particular place or situation, returning to it may trigger another attack or a fight-or-flight response. The person associates panic attacks with these places, and the memory of how distressed, unsafe and out of control they felt can leave them with a lack of confidence in being able to cope with it happening again. As a result they can develop agoraphobia and a dread of being in such places due to catastrophic fears and predictions that they could experience another sudden and extreme surge of panicky bodily symptoms and lose control. They worry that they will be incapacitated, trapped, humiliated and unable to escape to a safe place. The anxiety is usually accompanied by and exacerbated by intense fear that no one will come to their rescue and get them the help they need.

If a young person suffers with panic and agoraphobia, this can be extremely worrying and stressful for their parents/carers and limiting for their family as a whole. It can involve significant social isolation and lead to school disruption/refusal. If parents or carers notice that this type of avoidance is happening and is generalising to lots of places, it's important to seek evaluation at the earliest possible stage to determine if the fear of having panic attacks is the reason for the avoidance. Agoraphobic avoidance can become extreme, interfere with a young person's daily functioning and lead to depression, so early intervention is vital.

When a child or young person is distressed and refusing to leave their home, this can look like or be interpreted as other forms of anxiety such as social, separation or school anxiety. If a young person begins to suffer with panic attacks, it's important to be vigilant against the possibility that agoraphobia can develop. Criteria for diagnosis of agoraphobia include the person being fearful and anxious in at least two separate situations; the problem persisting for six months or more, and it causing significant distress and affecting their functioning socially, at school or in life in general.

On a positive note, there is good evidence to support the use of self-help resources and talking therapies such as Cognitive Behavioural Therapy (CBT) which includes exposure therapy for the treatment of panic with agoraphobia in children and young people, as recommended by the NHS.

Panic attacks case study: Ailsa, age 13

Ailsa had a gentle, quiet temperament, with a tendency to be shy and self-conscious. Her Panic Disorder had been triggered during a flight home from a family holiday when the aeroplane experienced extreme turbulence. This caused Ailsa to feel panicky and terrified that the plane would crash. She felt nauseous, becoming so frightened that she vomited. Ailsa found this incredibly embarrassing and distressing. She was trembling and burst into tears as soon as they landed.

Unfortunately, Ailsa continued to worry about having a panic attack on an aeroplane. This anxiety became generalised towards travelling on any form of public transport, which she began to avoid completely in case she felt such extreme anxiety again. Ailsa's family were very worried about her and believed that she was feeling down because she was missing out on fun outings with her friends. Her father was able to drive her to and from school, but this could have become a problem for the family in the longer term.

Ailsa's mother spoke to a friend who worked in mental health, who gave her a self-help guide to support Ailsa's recovery. If this was not effective, the family agreed that they would seek professional help.

Individual/idiosyncratic formulation: Ailsa

Anxious thoughts/cognitions	Anxious emotions
<ul><li>"This aeroplane is going to crash and we will all be killed."</li><li>"I feel so sick. My stomach is churning and I'm going to vomit with all these people around me."</li><li>"My body is shaking so badly I'm going to collapse."</li><li>"Everyone on the flight will see I'm anxious and will see me being sick."</li><li>"I need to get out, but I'm trapped in this cabin with all these people."</li><li>"They'll think I'm crazy and stupid."</li><li>"I can't breathe properly and my heart is thumping. There must be something wrong with me."</li><li>"I've lost control of myself. What's wrong with me?"</li></ul>	<ul><li>Terrified</li><li>Apprehensive</li><li>Panicky</li><li>Agitated and restless</li><li>Unable to concentrate</li><li>Feeling out of control</li><li>Exhausted</li><li>Feeling down; low mood</li></ul>
Physical symptoms of anxiety	Anxious behaviours
<ul><li>Nausea, stomach churning</li><li>Hyperventilation and shallow breathing</li><li>Heart racing or skipping a beat</li><li>Dizzy, lightheaded or faint</li><li>Shaky legs</li><li>Hands trembling</li><li>Dry mouth</li><li>Bodily tension</li><li>Poor sleep quality</li><li>Appetite disturbance; eating very little before going to school</li></ul>	<ul><li>Tearful, reluctant to go to school.</li><li>Avoiding travelling on any public transport due to concern about having a panic attack and being sick in front of others.</li><li>Frequently seeking reassurance that it will be OK.</li><li>Social withdrawal from friends; missing out on going into town with them on the bus.</li><li>Spending long periods worrying about having another attack.</li><li>Uncharacteristic irritability.</li><li>Decline in academic performance.</li><li>Issues with school punctuality; avoidance and refusal.</li></ul>

What helped Ailsa with her panic attacks?

Adopt and model a calm approach to the situation. Explain to the young person what you know about the problem and how it can feel, and normalise it. Identify the main issues and reasons for their worries.

For Ailsa, the mere thought of using public transport triggered some panic symptoms. She was convinced that getting so anxious and being physically sick meant that there was something seriously wrong with her. Her mother read the psychoeducational information she had been given about panic attacks and anxiety, and took a calm, matter-of-fact approach to what had happened. She explained the cycle of panic and that there were lots of ways to calm Ailsa's bodily symptoms to prevent them from escalating to the point of her vomiting. They talked about the fight-or-flight response, and how this prepares the body for danger even if there is no actual threat. She also explained that panic attacks are very common, are not dangerous, and do not last long before they subside. She told Ailsa that she knew of a family member who had experienced panic attacks and had learned to manage them so that they could go about their daily life without missing out on things. Ailsa seemed relieved and hopeful upon learning all of this.

Cultivate emotional awareness. Help the young person to identify and cope with their emotions. Show understanding and validate their feelings.

Ailsa and her mother talked about and normalised the feelings she was having. They acknowledged the fact that the physical symptoms of anxiety can be frightening, and that it was therefore not unnatural for Ailsa to feel this way. She was able to talk about feeling terrified and panicky, and about the intensity of her fear of losing control and vomiting. All of this had resulted in her feeling low and helpless. She felt a great sense of relief at being able to share her feelings without fear of judgement. This helped to reduce her sense of hopelessness and lower her anxiety.

Help the young person to learn and practise self-regulating and soothing coping strategies to manage symptoms. Adopt strategies for general wellbeing.

Ailsa learned to practise breathing techniques and calming visualisations of peaceful places. She tried these out with her mother at first, when she was not in situations that provoked her anxiety. She realised that the waves of panic and anxiety did subside on their own, and that breathing and positive self-talk were helpful in the moment. She also really enjoyed mindfulness exercises and practised these in the mornings and evenings. When asked to rate her anticipatory anxiety, she felt that the levels had come down significantly after a few weeks, and she felt a huge sense of achievement.

A helpful strategy if a child is having a panic attack is to reduce their focus on bodily symptoms. Ask them to bring their attention to something else in the immediate environment like a picture and to describe what they see. Alternatively, they could focus on something that brings them a sense of calm, such as talking about a family member or pet. Visualising a safe place is also a useful distraction while symptoms naturally subside. Ailsa found this very effective as it gave her a sense of control and helped her to feel less worried about her bodily symptoms. Her mother also helped her to install a meditation app on her phone for times of difficulty. Ailsa responded well to this and explored it at length to identify the areas she found most useful.

Help the young person to identify and challenge negative thoughts and worries. Develop alternative, more realistic thoughts and positive self-talk. Speak to them about the link between unhelpful thoughts, emotions and behaviours.

Ailsa's mother encouraged her to record her anxious and catastrophic thoughts in a thought diary. She then helped her to challenge these ideas and realise that they were disproportionate to reality. Ailsa also learned how common panic attacks are, and that other people would understand and not judge her. It was a relief for her to realise that Panic Disorder is a common condition, and that help and support are always available.

Help the young person to recognise and understand any unhelpful and avoidant behaviours. Talk about helping them to reduce symptoms by gradually facing their fears and trying to get back to enjoying life.

It was very important to begin to help Ailsa to overcome her fear of travelling on public transport. Her mother worked with her to agree a hierarchy of different types of transport, with aircraft at the top because this was the most difficult challenge for her to overcome. They knew that it would take time and had to be done at her own pace. They began by planning small, gradual steps towards travelling in the car. Then they moved on to travelling one stop on a bus together. When Ailsa had managed this several times without distress, they gradually increased the distance. Ailsa then progressed to travelling without her mother and was soon able to go to school on the bus with one of her friends. She eventually felt comfortable enough to travel both to and from school on the bus.

This gradual approach to reducing Ailsa's avoidance worked well, and her confidence was building. She was beginning to reclaim the things she had previously enjoyed. The bodily symptoms had reduced in intensity and, although she still had anxiety, she was tolerating her symptoms and feeling much more in control. She was also feeling hopeful and much happier.

How to help – panic attacks

- ☞ Educate yourself about panic attacks and anxiety and share what you have learned with the child to provide reassurance.

- ☞ Give the child the opportunity to share their experiences without fear of judgement. Normalise and validate their feelings.

- ☞ Explore self-soothing strategies and practise them when the child is not felling anxious. This can provide valuable coping techniques and reduce levels of anticipatory anxiety. Apps such as Headspace can provide effective tools for us in times of difficulty.

- ☞ Keeping a thought diary can be an excellent way to record, assess and challenge anxious or catastrophic thoughts.

- ☞ Help the child to recognise any avoidant behaviours that stem from their anxiety. Work together to overcome these habits in small steps.

- ☞ During a panic attack, encourage the child to direct their focus away from the bodily symptoms. They could concentrate on something else in the immediate environment and describe what they see, think about something that brings them a sense of calm, or visualise a safe place.

Chapter 18: Specific phobias

Phobias are very common, affecting around ten million people of different ages and genders in the UK alone.[78] Although there are many possible causes of phobias, the trigger can often be a particularly frightening episode. Phobias can also be learned from observing the behaviour of significant others. For example, a child may see a parent or sibling behaving anxiously around wasps and interpret these insects as hugely threatening. Other individuals may be genetically inclined towards anxiety and thus more likely to develop phobias. In general, people with specific phobias don't have wider anxiety issues or feel unsafe in the world; their fears are only around specific objects or situations.

> **Key Point**
>
> *In general, people with specific phobias don't have wider anxiety issues or feel unsafe in the world; their fears are only around specific objects or situations.*

Children can naturally go through stages of being scared and preoccupied by things like monsters, ghosts or scary films. Phobic anxiety, however, is more extreme and can cause high levels of distress. A specific phobia is defined as *"a marked fear or anxiety about a specific object or situation (for example, flying, heights, animals, receiving an injection, or seeing blood)."*[5] It is important to note that specific phobias are distinct from other more complex conditions that can also contain the word 'phobia' and which can have a more disruptive or incapacitating impact – for example social phobia (an alternative term for social anxiety, see Chapter 16) and agoraphobia (which is related to panic disorder – see Chapter 17).

Clinical research has suggested that gradual exposure to the feared object or situation is one of the most effective ways to treat phobias.[79] With mild to moderate phobias, this gradual exposure can usually be carried out effectively by the parents or carers. Further information on the effectiveness of exposure and response prevention can be found in Chapter 11.

---

78 NHS Inform (2021): *Phobias*. Available at: https://www.nhsinform.scot/illnesses-and-conditions/mental-health/phobias

79 Thing, C., Lim-Ashworth, N., Poh, B. & Lim, C.G. (2020). Recent developments in the intervention of specific phobia among adults: a rapid review. *F1000Research* 9 F1000 Faculty Rev-195.

General features and symptoms

The following are examples of common types of specific phobia in children and young people. For individuals with a specific phobia, coming into contact with what frightens them causes intense fear and panic.

- Animal phobias: Fear of cats, dogs, spiders (arachnophobia), snakes (ophidiophobia) and insects such as wasps.
- Environmental phobias: Fear of being in water (hydrophobia), the dark (nyctophobia), thunder and lightning storms (astraphobia) and heights (acrophobia).
- Situational phobias: Fear of being alone (autophobia), going to the doctor or dentist, flying in aircraft (aerophobia), being in lifts or small confined spaces (claustrophobia), and travelling on escalators.
- Body-based phobias: Fear of vomiting (emetophobia), injections (trypanophobia), blood (haemophobia), and swallowing or choking.[80]

Other phobias can be related to certain foods, objects such as balloons, or costumed characters you might see at parties or funfairs. Specific phobias can trigger negative and unhelpful thoughts, extreme anxiety, panic attacks, and irrational fears of things that don't pose any real or significant danger. The feelings of anxiety and the need to avoid these objects or situations can be extreme and enduring. Phobic anxiety can considerably interfere with a child or young person's psychological wellbeing and ability to function normally in day-to-day social or school environments.

Specific phobia case study: Kieran, age 7

Kieran had experienced a balloon bursting in his face at a birthday party the previous year. The noise and proximity terrified him, and it resulted in him screaming and running to his mother. He was crying and said that he wanted to leave the party. His mother could see his distress and took him home. Kieran was inconsolable for quite some time that day, and for a couple of weeks afterwards he had trouble getting to sleep at night because he kept thinking about the incident.

In the weeks that followed, Kieran received two more birthday party invitations. He refused to go, and his parents didn't force him because they could see that he was extremely upset at the prospect of going to birthday parties and encountering balloons. Kieran had always loved school fetes and funfairs, but as these kinds of events approached, he

---

80 Mind: *Phobias*. Available at: https://www.mind.org.uk/information-support/types-of-mental-health-problems/phobias/types-of-phobia/

told his mother that he couldn't go because there would be balloons "everywhere". Kieran's parents were becoming worried about him because he was missing out on celebrations with friends and could not even contemplate having the customary balloons at his own birthday party. They realised that Kieran's fear was affecting him significantly and restricting the family in terms of places they could go to at weekends and in school holidays. They were beginning to think that they might need some help from an experienced professional.

Around the same time, Kieran went to watch a play at the theatre with his grandmother. During the performance, a boy who had a balloon on the other side of the aisle let it go and unfortunately it drifted across to where Kieran could see it. Kieran jumped up and bolted for the door. He ran out into the street before his grandmother was able to catch up with him. This caused great concern for the family about Kieran's safety and wellbeing, as he could have run out in front of a car. His mother was referred to a therapist who was experienced in dealing with phobias.

Kieran and his mother worked together with the therapist. The treatment initially involved psychoeducation about phobias for Kieran's mother, and later for both of them together. The therapist assessed Kieran's anxiety and produced an individual case formulation to guide the treatment process.

Individual/idiosyncratic formulation: Kieran

Anxious thoughts/cognitions	Anxious emotions
- "What if I go somewhere and I see balloons? I will freak out." - "Balloons are dangerous and harmful. I cannot be near them. They always burst." - "If they burst, they will make a loud bang and hurt my face." - "They always have them at parties and school fun days." - "I will lose control." - "I'm a cry baby for running away." - "People will see me and think I'm stupid and a cry baby." - "I can't go to parties and school fun days ever again." - "It's not fair." - "None of my friends are frightened. They will make fun of me."	- Apprehensive - Terrified and panicky - Constantly on alert and unsettled - Tense, on edge - Feeling out of control - Tired - Sad - Feeling down and miserable - Helpless - Hopeless
Physical symptoms of anxiety	Anxious behaviours
- Jumpy and easily startled - Hyperventilating - Heart beating fast - Body trembling - Stomach churning - Nausea - Tense - Easily irritated - Exhausted	- Avoiding situations out of fear of encountering balloons - Crying, high levels of distress, and refusal to go to places where there could be balloons - Running away if unexpectedly faced with balloons - Avoiding talking or thinking about balloons - Distress and need for a great deal of reassurance before going anywhere with family - Avoiding socialising with friends and missing out on fun activities - Quiet and withdrawn at school; not his usual bubbly and enthusiastic self

What helped Kieran with his specific phobia?

Adopt and model a calm approach to the situation. Explain to the young person what you know about the problem and how it can feel, and normalise it. Identify the main issues and reasons for their worries.

The therapist explained to Kieran that what he was feeling was anxiety, and that this is very common in adults, children and young people. She told him that phobias can result from frightening episodes, and helped him to understand that because he had had such a fright from what happened, it was no wonder that he was worried about coming into contact with balloons again. The therapist told Kieran that he was not stupid or weak to feel that way, and that it was natural to be scared.

Kieran's automatic negative prediction was that if he encountered a balloon again, it would most certainly burst in his face and cause him injury. It was important to help him learn that this was unrealistic and unlikely to happen. Nonetheless, it was understandable that he felt anxious and panicky after such a traumatic event. The therapist explained the fight-or-flight response, and that what Kieran was experiencing was a false alarm. She went on to reassure him that phobias can get better, and that she and his mother would be there to help him to recover.

Cultivate emotional awareness. Help the young person to identify and cope with their emotions. Show understanding and validate their feelings.

The therapist went through a list of emotions that people often feel if they have anxious and fearful thoughts about bad things happening. Using a book about anxiety and emotions, she helped Kieran to name his feelings by pointing to pictures of children's faces with words written underneath them. This helped Kieran to talk about his feelings, and to understand that he had gone through a scary experience that would naturally provoke difficult emotions. He identified feeling terrified, panicky and out of control even at the thought of a balloon. He felt sad that he was unable to go to birthday parties or amusement parks, because he was missing out on fun opportunities due to his fear of balloons.

The therapist went on to explain to Kieran that the fight-or-flight response could trigger strong physical reactions. She showed him a picture of the symptoms that people can often feel in their bodies. Kieran pointed to the ones that he was experiencing. Then, using a diagram of a body, Kieran used coloured pencils to write down his symptoms and draw arrows pointing to the areas where he felt the sensations. He then rated each one by intensity. The strongest symptoms Kieran felt were irregular breathing, heart pounding, trembling, tension, stomach churning and nausea. The therapist reassured him that she could teach him techniques to calm and manage these feelings.

Kieran shed a few tears during this process, but said he felt better having been able to tell someone else about what he was experiencing. He felt understood, and it was evident that his mother and the therapist did not think he was just being a silly baby. They praised him for being brave, and his mother gave him lots of big hugs.

Help the young person to learn and practise self-regulating and soothing coping strategies to manage symptoms. Adopt strategies for general wellbeing.

The next step for Kieran was to learn calming techniques to cope with the symptoms of his anxiety. He learned diaphragmatic breathing to combat the rapid breathing, progressive muscle relaxation to soothe bodily tension, and guided meditations to calm the body and mind. He enjoyed choosing and practising these techniques, and his favourite visualisation was lying on warm sand on a tropical island with the sun shining down, listening to the sound of the waves.

Kieran loved to ride his bike, and the family began to go on more frequent rides in the countryside to boost his physical activity. He also enjoyed playing football, and this was encouraged at school during break times. At home, Kieran's friends were invited for sleepovers and to play football in the garden to ensure that he was getting sufficient exercise, fun and social contact. Kieran seemed much happier and more engaged with his friends and family.

Kieran's class teacher arranged for him to be allowed to go and speak with the pastoral lead if he was feeling overwhelmed in school. The school also had a quiet room that Kieran could go to, equipped with a CD player and a range of calming audio meditations that he could use if he felt the need. Kieran had always enjoyed school and was very happy about this. He felt supported by the staff and more relaxed.

Help the young person to identify and challenge negative thoughts and worries. Develop alternative, more realistic thoughts and positive self-talk. Speak to them about the link between unhelpful thoughts, emotions and behaviours.

Kieran was able to reframe his anxious thoughts in the following ways.

Catastrophising:	"Balloons are dangerous and harmful."
Alternative:	"I had a bad experience when I was young. Balloons do burst and that can be scary, but I wasn't physically hurt. Realistically, bursting balloons won't hurt me."
Catastrophising:	"I'll cry and run away. I'll never be able to cope."
Alternative:	"This is anxiety, which is normal. I am learning ways to calm myself when I'm afraid and I know that balloons may not be as dangerous as I first thought."
Generalising:	"Balloons always burst."
Alternative:	"This is actually untrue, and realistically it is unlikely that I will have the same experience every time I'm close to balloons."
Fortune-telling:	"I can't go to parties and fun places ever again."
Alternative:	"The therapist will help me to gradually be able to do these things again. I have help and support to do this in small steps. I hope that if I'm brave, I'll get better."
Mind-reading:	"People will think I'm stupid and a cry baby."
Alternative:	"Phobias are common, and people know that they can cause high levels of anxiety. They are more likely to be kind and understanding and want to help."
Negative self-talk:	"I'm a cry baby for running away."
Alternatives:	"This is anxiety and I'm not a cry baby. I had a really bad experience." "People understand what I'm feeling and are helping me to get better. I can do it. I will be brave. I can take it step by step."

Help the young person to recognise and understand any unhelpful and avoidant behaviours. Talk about helping them to reduce symptoms by gradually facing their fears and trying to get back to enjoying life.

A key strategy to help Kieran to overcome his phobic avoidance and get back to normal was graded exposure to balloons in his environment. The therapist and Kieran's mother helped him put together a hierarchy ladder showing the situations he felt he could begin to face to try to tolerate his anxiety. They listed these from the easiest to the most difficult, which was attending a party or fun activity that could involve balloons. The steps had to be gradual and repeated until Kieran was ready to move up the ladder.[81]

Kieran was courageous and willing to begin his journey. Despite a few initial stops and starts, he persevered and completed the steps. After a few meetings with the therapist, Kieran and his family worked through the process themselves with an occasional booster and review session. Importantly, after each step in his recovery, Kieran's parents acknowledged how brave and determined he was and rewarded him for his efforts. Kieran was eventually able to be in the general vicinity of balloons. He still felt uncomfortable, but he was able to tolerate his anxiety so that he could enjoy himself and not miss out on fun activities.

---

[81] Anxiety Canada: *Self-Help: Managing Your Phobia*. Available at: https://www.anxietycanada.com/sites/default/files/adult_hmspecific.pdf

How to help – specific phobias

☞ Make use of self-help resources or professional support to learn about phobias and what the child may be experiencing. Help them to understand that anxiety is common and that phobias are a natural response to frightening episodes. Normalise what they are experiencing, and reassure them that they can overcome their phobia and you are there to support them.

☞ Help the child to identify the feelings and bodily symptoms that they are experiencing as a result of their anxiety. There are workbooks available to facilitate this process – please see the Appendix for some suggestions. Show empathy and understanding, and praise their courage in sharing what they have been experiencing.

☞ Introduce the child to various calming techniques to help them cope with the symptoms of their anxiety. Help them to practise these and identify the ones that they find most helpful. Encourage the child to engage in more healthy activities that will boost their overall wellbeing such as physical exercise, fun and social contact.

☞ Make the child's school aware of the challenges they are facing if some support would be appropriate. Accommodations can be made for specific challenges, and pastoral staff can be available as needed.

☞ Help the child to identify any unhelpful thoughts that they are having in relation to their anxiety. Work together to develop more realistic thoughts and positive self-talk affirmations that can be used to challenge and overcome negative thinking patterns.

☞ Support the child in gradually facing their fears and phobic avoidance so that they can get back to enjoying life again. This can be achieved through graded exposure to the source of their anxiety by planning achievable steps with the child. Offer praise for their progress and support through any setbacks.

Part 4: Other forms of anxiety less common in children and young people

Chapter 19: Post-Traumatic Stress Disorder (PTSD)

Children and young people can witness or be involved in traumatic or life-threatening events that can result in emotional disturbance and distress. Examples include serious accidents, violent acts and natural disasters. This form of trauma-related anxiety is known as Post-Traumatic Stress Disorder (PTSD). House fires,

> *Key Point*
>
> *Children can often make a natural recovery from traumatic events with the support of family and the people around them.*

accidents in the home, or being bitten by a dog or other animal can have a similar impact.[82] It is important to understand that children can also be traumatised if they are frequently exposed to frightening reports and images via the news or social media. It is reassuring to know, however, that they can often make a natural recovery from these traumatic events with the support of family and the people around them.[83]

One form of traumatic event that has very much come to the fore in recent years is a health crisis. Good quality evidence about the impact and traumatic effects of the COVID-19 pandemic on children and young people's mental health is still being gathered. So far, indications suggest that it has taken a significant toll.[84] It is important to understand and recognise the emotional difficulties that our young people could be experiencing, and to maintain an ongoing awareness of and lookout for trauma symptoms.

General features and symptoms

Traumatic stress is a natural response to frightening and threatening events. However, it can create intense and overwhelming physical, emotional and behavioural difficulties. PTSD can have negative effects on a child or young person's psychological wellbeing and functioning. It can lead to low mood, sleep and appetite disturbance, isolation, and

---

82 Smith, P., Perrin, S., Yule, W. & Clark, D.M. (2010) *Post-Traumatic Stress Disorder: Cognitive Therapy with Children and Young People (1st ed.)*. London: Routledge.

83 HelpGuide: *Helping Children Cope with Traumatic Events*. Available at: https://www.helpguide.org/articles/ptsd-trauma/helping-children-cope-with-traumatic-stress.htm

84 Douglas, P., Douglas, D., Harrigan, D., Douglas, K. (2009) Preparing for pandemic influenza and its aftermath: Mental health issues considered. *International Journal of Emergency Mental Health* 11 137-44.

feelings of helplessness and being unsafe. Additional support may be necessary if a young person has a pre-existing anxiety or mood condition, or has experienced previous trauma in their lives. This is due to a greater vulnerability to more severe and enduring stress reactions to trauma.

The Ehlers and Clark model of PTSD proposes that the brain does not process memory properly following a traumatic incident.[85] Instead, it remains in a constant state of hypervigilance to the threat that has been experienced. Any memory cues or reminders can trigger the same level of distress and the feeling that the incident is happening again in the moment. This is because the part of the brain that controls memory and helps us to determine the chronology of events (*hippocampus*), and those parts that help us to reason and regulate our emotions (*amygdala*) and control our behaviour (*prefrontal cortex*) do not function as they normally would. Our brain therefore tells us that the threat is still present rather than being in the past.[86]

Children and young people who are experiencing PTSD are likely to struggle to varying degrees with some or all of the problems below. The particular difficulties and symptoms will be unique to each individual case.

Fear and anxiety

Following a traumatic event, children can experience extreme fear if they are reminded in any way of what happened. This could take the form of anything associated with the event, such as being near to the scene or encountering something that brings back memories of what they went through. Certain objects, sounds or smells can trigger an automatic fear response. The young person can feel unsafe in the world, not want to be on their own and become hyperalert to danger, constantly worrying that the same thing could happen to them or their loved ones again.

Flashbacks and re-experiencing memories

A young person with PTSD can experience uncontrolled, repetitive memories and images of the traumatic event. These can be extremely vivid and distressing, like a video playing over and over in the mind. Since trauma interferes with the organisation of memory, there may be some parts of the traumatic event that the young person does not recall.

---

[85] Ehlers, A. & Clark, D.M. (2000). A cognitive model of posttraumatic stress disorder. *Behaviour Research and Therapy* 38 (4), 319–345.

[86] Goodall, B., Chadwick, I., McKinnon, A., Werner-Seidler, A., Meiser-Stedman, R., Smith, P. & Dalgleish, T. (2017), Translating the Cognitive Model of PTSD to the Treatment of Very Young Children: A Single Case Study of an 8-Year-Old Motor Vehicle Accident Survivor. *Journal of Clinical Psychology* 73 511-523.

They may also suffer with nightmares. During a flashback, they can feel as if what they are experiencing is real and happening again and undergo the same level of terror that they felt during the original trauma. This can be isolating for young people if they don't tell anyone what is happening to them. They can be terrified that they are going mad, which is not the case – it is simply the way in which our brain reacts to trauma. Explaining this to a young person can provide enormous relief and reassurance.

Hyperarousal and physical symptoms

A common and natural response to trauma usually involves severe physical anxiety symptoms as the body prepares for fight or flight. Young people with PTSD can be constantly alert and feel jumpy, on edge, unable to relax, nauseous, shaky and tense. They can experience significant sleep disturbance, nightmares, and changes in their usual appetite. They may also frequently complain of stomach aches or headaches.

Avoidance

Any reminders or memory cues relating to the trauma can create high levels of fear, and consequently the child or young person with PTSD will try very hard to avoid anything they associate with the event. The distress and re-experiencing that are triggered mean that they may avoid ever talking about what happened, and even try to stop themselves from thinking or having any sort of feelings about it.

When to seek professional help

If the trauma-related anxiety persists for more than a month, it is best to seek support and assessment from your GP, who if appropriate can make a referral to mental health professionals. Signs that PTSD symptoms are taking hold can vary greatly. Very young children may become clingy and anxious, have tantrums, or begin wetting the bed. Older children may appear angry or easily irritated, isolate themselves, or start to perform worse academically.

The symptoms of PTSD can lead to helplessness and hopelessness if the child or teenager internalises the traumatic distress and withdraws from friends and family. Depression is commonly associated with having PTSD, and if the young person is suffering with both conditions, treatment could be essential. Please see Part 5 for more information on depression. It is important to understand how this can develop as a result of prolonged anxiety, and to be able to spot the warning signs as early as possible.

Post-Traumatic Stress Disorder (PTSD) case study: Leanne, age 14

Leanne had been travelling in her father's car when another driver ran a red light and crashed into one of the rear doors, causing them to spin around in the road. Fortunately, Leanne was seated on the opposite side of the car in the front passenger seat, and nobody was harmed. However, Leanne was very shaken and had been extremely afraid that she or her father would be seriously hurt or killed. The damage to the vehicle was repaired quickly, but Leanne was too frightened to travel by car again. Despite some anxiety, she could cope with travelling to school by bus as she felt that there would be less damage and harm to the passengers in an accident.

For two to three weeks after the accident, Leanne experienced severe anxiety and panic symptoms at the thought of getting into a car. When anything reminded her of what had taken place, she felt like it was happening again and had vivid images in her mind of the accident. During the crash she had heard a loud bang as the cars collided, and she would now become startled and distressed if she heard a loud noise when she was out and about or watching television. She didn't want to discuss the accident, saying that she just wanted to forget everything. She hadn't been sleeping well following the trauma, but this seemed to improve after around three weeks.

Individual/idiosyncratic formulation: Leanne

Anxious thoughts/cognitions	Anxious emotions
■ "I can't get it out of my head." ■ "It feels like I'm back there and it's happening all over again." ■ "It feels real: I can see it happening." ■ "I'm going mad. It keeps popping up in my head and I can't control it." ■ "I must be vigilant all the time in case it happens again." ■ "Will I ever feel normal again?" ■ "I'm weak and pathetic, and I'll never get over it." ■ "I can't control it – my body won't stop shaking and I feel so sick. There's something wrong with me." ■ "I can't tell my parents or friends. They'll think I've lost my mind."	■ Extremely anxious ■ Terrified ■ Tense and hypervigilant ■ On edge and restless ■ Distressed but not able to cry ■ Emotionally numb ■ Irritable and angry ■ Unable to concentrate ■ Disconnected and isolated from family and friends ■ Helpless ■ Pessimistic ■ Low mood/depressed ■ Lack of interest or motivation to engage in usual activities
Physical symptoms of anxiety	Anxious behaviours
■ Jumpy and easily startled ■ Hyperventilation ■ Tightness in chest ■ Heart racing ■ Body trembling ■ Nausea ■ Poor appetite ■ Poor quality of sleep and difficulty in getting to sleep ■ Low energy	■ Trying to avoid thoughts and feelings about the accident. ■ Fear and avoidance of talking about the accident. ■ Avoiding being in or near her father's car or anything that triggers the memory. ■ Extremely startled and distressed upon hearing loud bangs. ■ Displaying distress if asked to travel in the car. ■ Not engaging socially as she normally would. ■ Withdrawing from family and friends ■ Spending time alone in her bedroom worrying.

What helped Leanne with her PTSD?

Adopt and model a calm approach to the situation. Explain to the young person what you know about the problem and how it can feel, and normalise it. Identify the main issues and reasons for their worries.

Leanne's parents didn't pressure her into talking about the accident, but they did say that it could help her to feel better when she was ready. About a month later, Leanne was able to talk to her father about what had happened. They discussed their feelings and reactions to the accident. Her father had read up on PTSD and trauma responses. He was able to explain to her how trauma can affect the brain and cause such distress. He shared his own reactions with Leanne, which helped her to understand what had been happening to her and normalised her experiences. This was a great help, and Leanne felt relieved and reassured that her reactions did not mean that she was going mad. Talking through what had happened allowed Leanne to process the memory with her father. This enabled her to find perspective, and to recognise that the accident was in the past. Processing the trauma memory can often help to reduce re-experiencing.

Cultivate emotional awareness. Help the young person to identify and cope with their emotions. Show understanding and validate their feelings.

Leanne was able to disclose how anxious and on edge she had been feeling whenever thoughts of the accident suddenly came into her mind. It seemed like this would continue forever, and she felt helpless, out of control and afraid to talk about it. Leanne's parents helped her to express her emotions and reactions to the accident. They showed care and understanding of how such a trauma could cause her to feel so frightened and anxious.

Help the young person to learn and practise self-regulating and soothing coping strategies to manage symptoms. Adopt strategies for general wellbeing.

Having gained an understanding of the symptoms and difficulties that Leanne was experiencing, the next step was for her to learn and practise calming and self-soothing techniques. Leanne found these effective when dealing with the overwhelming anxiety and physical symptoms. She practised grounding and stabilising techniques, breathing exercises, progressive muscle relaxation and guided visualisations.

Leanne had always enjoyed music, dance, swimming and other healthy ways to relax. She was encouraged to take these up again as often as was practical, and to gradually begin to socialise more with her friends. These activities really helped Leanne to put the accident behind her. Over time her emotional wellbeing improved. She began to feel happier and less anxious, and she was able to resume life as normal.

Help the young person to identify and challenge negative thoughts and worries. Develop alternative, more realistic thoughts and positive self-talk. Speak to them about the link between unhelpful thoughts, emotions and behaviours.

It took some time to encourage and help Leanne to talk about the worries and negative thoughts she had about herself, others, and the future and to help her to find more realistic and balanced perspectives. She said that she found this challenging, but it helped her to feel less anxious and more positive about herself and what she had been through. She was able to reframe her thoughts in the following ways.

Catastrophising:	"It's happening again. I'm going mad. I'm losing control. I'll never feel normal again."
Alternative:	"That's what trauma feels like. It's awful but it's normal, and I'll get over this."
Catastrophising:	"The world isn't safe. I need to be constantly alert."
Alternative:	"I'm safe now, it's in the past. These things don't happen all the time."
Emotional reasoning and fortune-telling:	"If I feel like this, something bad is bound to happen."
Alternative:	"Trauma makes you feel that way, but feelings are not facts. It's a stress reaction."
Labelling and self-criticism:	"I'm weak and pathetic."
Alternative:	"It was a brave step to begin to tell Mum and Dad how bad I was feeling. I've been through an awful ordeal, and I now have the support to get better."
Positive self-talk:	"It's in the past, and Dad and I are safe now. I've been brave. I'm getting back to normal again. I wasn't going mad; that' how trauma affects people and I can recover."

Help the young person to recognise and understand any unhelpful and avoidant behaviours. Talk about helping them to reduce symptoms by gradually facing their fears and trying to get back to enjoying life.

Leanne's parents could understand her avoidant behaviours, but they recognised that these would actually perpetuate and prolong her anxiety. Avoidance maintains the person's overestimation of threat and their underestimation of being able to cope.

Gradually, Leanne and her parents began the process of exposure to being in the car. Close family members helped to encourage and facilitate the process. Leanne began by looking at the car, then standing next to it in the driveway. She then progressed to sitting in her father and mother's cars without driving anywhere. She was eventually able to make very short journeys. The plan was then to gradually increase the duration of the car journeys to improve Leanne's confidence in her ability to cope. It was key to do this at a pace that she was able to tolerate.

How to help – Post-Traumatic Stress Disorder (PTSD)

☞ Don't put the child under any pressure to talk about the traumatic event that has caused their anxiety. Let them know that you are available to talk when they are ready.

☞ Take some time to learn about PTSD so that you can understand how trauma affects the brain and the impact it may be having on the child. Share what you have learned to normalise what they are experiencing and help them to understand it.

☞ Give the child the opportunity to explore and process their feelings and reactions to the trauma. Show empathy and validate the anxiety that has resulted from the experience.

☞ Help the child to practise and implement various calming and self-soothing techniques to relieve their anxiety and physical symptoms. Encourage them to take up other healthy activities to help them relax and improve their general wellbeing, such as playing sports and spending time with friends.

☞ Work with the child to explore any negative and unhelpful thoughts and to find more realistic and balanced perspectives. Encourage them to reframe the negative thoughts by identifying and focusing on more helpful alternatives.

☞ Help the child to recognise any avoidant behaviours and think about ways in which these can be reduced so that they can enjoy life again. Work with them to plan a gradual exposure to the trigger(s) of their anxiety. It is crucial to do this, and equally important to work at a pace that they can tolerate. Offer plenty of support and encouragement along the way.

☞ If the trauma-related anxiety persists for more than a month, it is best to seek support and assessment. It is important to be aware that PTSD is commonly associated with depression, and to be able to spot the warning signs as early as possible. If the child is suffering with both conditions, treatment could be essential.

Chapter 20: Obsessive-Compulsive Disorder (OCD)

Obsessive-Compulsive Disorder (OCD) is a less common type of anxiety that is thought to affect between one and two percent of children and young people. Symptoms can begin in childhood, and identification at the earliest possible stage is important to ensure that the young person receives the appropriate treatment or help to manage their condition.

Expert View

"OCD is characterised by obsessive thoughts and compulsive behaviours which significantly interfere with everyday functioning."

Tim Williams and Polly Waite[87]

Precisely what causes OCD is not yet certain, but factors that may be involved include genetics, learned behaviour, and a biological imbalance in brain chemistry – particularly a deficit in a neurotransmitter called serotonin. Those with a predisposition may find that OCD is triggered by adverse life events such as a death in the family or a parental divorce, or by certain illnesses. OCD generally involves obsessive intrusive thoughts and a disproportionate sense of responsibility for the safety of others.

General features and symptoms

Although it can begin in childhood, OCD tends to become more evident in the early teens and adulthood. Some young people may have mild symptoms that do not significantly impact on their daily lives.

OCD can be more easily understood if we break it down into its two main characteristics: obsessive thoughts and compulsive behaviours.[88]

- **Obsessive thoughts:** Intrusive, recurring thoughts, scary impulses or images can enter the minds of people with OCD. These can be very distressing and difficult to control, causing the person to feel compelled to react to protect themselves and their loved ones.

---

[87] Waite, P., & Williams, T. (eds.) (2009) *Obsessive Compulsive Disorder: Cognitive Behaviour Therapy with Children and Young People.* London: Routledge.

[88] Salkovskis, P.M., Forrester, E. & Richards, C. (1998) Cognitive–behavioural approach to understanding obsessional thinking. *The British Journal of Psychiatry*, 173(S35), 53-63.

- **Compulsive behaviours:** People with OCD can feel compelled to engage in repetitive actions or rituals to try to prevent bad things happening, to calm the anxiety caused by obsessive disturbing thoughts, or to neutralise or banish them. Some compulsions are physical, while others can be carried out mentally and may not be observable behaviours.

Common obsessions in children and young people

- **Contamination:** Obsessive fear of germs, feeling dirty and contamination.
- **Illness:** Extreme fear of self or family members catching viruses and becoming ill or dying.
- **Harm:** Obsessive fear of harm occurring to self or loved ones.
- **Morality and religion:** Extreme fear of having intrusive thoughts and impulses, contrary to the individual's moral or religious beliefs, about causing harm to others. This can also include experiencing unwanted sexual or violent thoughts, images or urges. People with OCD are extremely unlikely to act on such thoughts as they are so distressing, and will go to great lengths to prevent them happening.
- **Magical thinking:** Exaggerated sense of responsibility for ensuring the safety and wellbeing of self and loved ones. People with OCD can have strong beliefs that thinking and acting in specific ways will achieve this. They can believe that certain numbers, words, colours or alignments of objects have special powers. They may also avoid what they believe are unlucky numbers, colours, words and places.

Common compulsions in children and young people

- **Cleaning:** Frequent wiping, washing hands or showering. Feeling compelled to repeat these actions until clean or safe enough. This can take a long time and have a negative effect on the skin.
- **Avoiding:** Staying away from places which could be dirty or harbour germs. For example crowds, medical settings or public toilets. Also contact with chemicals, door handles, money or others' hands.
- **Checking:** Repeatedly making sure that things are turned off or secure, such as doors, windows, electrical appliances and taps.
- **Repeating compulsions:** Ensuring that things are done correctly and in the same way. For example, writing and re-writing homework, or tapping objects or parts of the body an exact number of times.

- **Need for order and symmetry:** Making sure that things feel 'just right' or perfect. For example, keeping things neat and tidy or putting them in an exact order or arrangement.

The purpose of all these rituals is to feel calmer and prevent feared catastrophes. However, the desperate need to engage in multiple rituals can be exhausting and distressing, and hugely disruptive to the quality of day-to-day life for both the young person and their family.

- **Family life:** Trying to care for your child and witnessing the distress caused by OCD can be anxiety-provoking and exhausting for parents. Compulsive behaviours can dominate family life and cause frustration for siblings, resulting in family discord.[89]
- **School life:** Compulsions can interfere with school punctuality and attendance. Distracting thoughts can cause problems with learning and concentration, hampering academic progress.
- **Social functioning:** Interacting with peers and maintaining friendships may be problematic for the young person because others may not understand their rigid, rule-orientated behaviours, and may respond unkindly.

It is important to be aware that young people may experience mental compulsions that cannot be seen. Obsessions are often internalised and not disclosed to parents or professionals. Young children may not even realise that their worries are unrealistic. Some young people can feel embarrassed or ashamed about having 'weird' obsessive thoughts and compulsive behaviours, and therefore keep them hidden until such time as they becomes obvious to others.

Depending on circumstances, it can be useful for parents and carers to connect with support groups and talk to other parents of children suffering with OCD. These forums can be a fantastic source of support and shared experience. There are also websites and charities relating to OCD which can help you to understand and know how best to support your child.

---

89 NHS (2020) *Helping Your Child with OCD – A Parent / Carer Self Help Guide.* Available at: https://www.anxietyuk.org.uk/wp-content/uploads/2020/10/Helpling-your-child-with-Obsessive-Compulsive-Disorder.pdf

OCD in the school environment

Confiding in key people at school can be very helpful for young people with OCD and their parents. If rituals are being performed in school, it's helpful to make staff aware of the difficulties and anxiety that OCD can cause. It's useful for them to know how you are approaching the condition, and the strategies you are using at home. School staff can also be watchful, and let you know if they feel that your child is experiencing problems with peers or friendships which could be affecting their self-esteem or causing low mood.

Due to OCD, the young person may have difficulties regarding school such as punctuality caused by tiredness or needing to perform time consuming rituals before they leave the home. Sometimes there can be school refusal, perhaps due to worry around being separated from family and something bad happening. Poor concentration is common due to anxiety; allowing extra time to complete tasks is a simple and helpful accommodation.

Obsessive-Compulsive Disorder (OCD) case study: Akira, age 12

Akira was a sensitive, caring girl who had shown anxious tendencies from an early age. She seemed to be preoccupied about anything bad happening to her family, and could be quite clingy. Her parents gradually realised that she was regularly checking things around the house to make sure they were secure or switched off in case of a burglary or fire. Akira's mother wondered if it might have been caused by something she had seen on television. It became clear that this was more than just a minor concern for Akira, and it was escalating.

Akira's father was able to sit her down and ask her how she was feeling. She felt disproportionately responsible for ensuring that everything was safe in the house, even though she knew that her parents were responsible for this. She was spending increasing amounts of time checking and re-checking doors, windows, electrical appliances and the house alarm. If this was interrupted or stopped, she would become distressed. Her mother had not prevented her from doing the checks as they seemed to help her to calm down. However, they were now taking up to an hour or longer.

Akira also seemed to have a particular 'lucky number' of times she would carry out the checks, and believed that if she didn't follow this she would be responsible for bad things happening. She had mental images of the house burning down, and of burglars damaging the home and taking their possessions. She would frequently text her mother when she was working from home to check if everything was OK. The rituals she had to engage in were beginning to impact her and her siblings getting to school on time. Her younger brother was sometimes scared of how frantic she would be, and became upset when she cried. Her older sister was less understanding, which caused frequent family arguments. Akira reached a point where she didn't want to talk about it, saying that they would not understand and would think she was insane if she told them how bad things were.

Akira's mother was overwhelmed and very worried, and she contacted the school therapist. This therapist was an experienced practitioner who had worked with young people with OCD and anxiety. Akira agreed to speak to her and was happy for her mother to be included. The therapist assessed and formulated what was happening to Akira, and shared this with her and her mother to clarify what was happening. She explained the nature of OCD, and helped Akira to map out her thoughts, feelings and behaviours.

Chapter 20: Obsessive-Compulsive Disorder (OCD)

Individual/idiosyncratic formulation: Akira

Anxious thoughts/cognitions	Anxious emotions
■ "What if bad things happen?" ■ "I must make sure our home is safe and secure." ■ "If I get things wrong, there could be a fire or burglary and my family could get hurt." ■ "If I check the doors, windows and appliances, then I have protected my family." ■ "To be sure I've done the checks properly, I must do them eight times at night and in the morning." ■ "I must not get this wrong. It will be my fault if I don't do everything I can to keep us safe from harm." ■ Mind racing, experiencing distressing thoughts and images of a fire or burglary and of her family being hurt.	■ tense ■ worried all the time ■ uncertain that the home is safe ■ apprehensive ■ nervous ■ unsettled ■ agitated ■ on edge, easily startled ■ unable to relax ■ poor concentration at school ■ exhausted ■ unhappy and tearful ■ unable to enjoy things ■ lonely
Physical symptoms of anxiety	Anxious behaviours
■ trembling ■ sweating ■ over-breathing ■ heart racing ■ nausea ■ light-headed ■ poor appetite ■ difficulty getting to sleep; waking at night and unable to get back to sleep ■ tired and low energy	■ hypervigilant of house security ■ checking doors, windows, alarm, plugs, appliances for long periods at bedtime and before school ■ frequently texting Mum at home for reassurance that her checks worked and everyone is safe ■ tearful and distressed if prevented from carrying out rituals ■ ruminating and worrying ■ unhappy and anxious; not wanting to leave the house ■ hypervigilant about anything going wrong ■ avoiding talking about worries ■ distress when asked about worries ■ checking everyone is happy and OK ■ unable to sit and settle for long

What helped Akira with her OCD?

Adopt and model a calm approach to the situation. Explain to the young person what you know about the problem and how it can feel, and normalise it. Identify the main issues and reasons for their worries.

The therapist's assessment determined that Akira was suffering with quite severe OCD. In collaboration with Akira and her mother, she recommended a self-help book to guide the strategies that they would use in therapy and at home.[90] The therapy focused on managing anxiety by identifying and working with Akira's obsessional thoughts and compulsive rituals.

The therapist described the nature of OCD, particularly obsessions and compulsions. She explained that OCD is a well-known problem that can be treated, and that some children and young people do not disclose their obsessive thoughts to others for fear of judgement. Talking about OCD helped Akira to share what she had been experiencing.

The therapist explained to Akira's mother that if you can help a child to tell you what their obsessive thoughts are, and what these thoughts compel them to do, then this is a huge step forward. It is important to stay calm and not look alarmed. Educate yourself and your child about OCD, and explain that the fact that they have the condition is not their fault.

Cultivate emotional awareness. Help the young person to identify and cope with their emotions. Show understanding and validate their feelings.

The therapist and Akira's mother helped Akira to talk about the feelings she was having, and responded compassionately to her distress. Akira disclosed that she had been feeling constantly worried, on edge and unsettled. She felt that the only way she could feel less anxious was by performing the rituals, but then the uncertainty would return and it would start all over again. She had been feeling exhausted, alone in her fears and unhappy for a very long time.

---

[90] March, J.S., & Benton, C.M. (2006). *Talking Back to OCD: The Program That Helps Kids and Teens Say "No Way" – and Parents Say "Way to Go"*. New York, Guilford Press.

Help the young person to learn and practise self-regulating and soothing coping strategies to manage symptoms. Adopt strategies for general wellbeing.

Akira learned how to shift her attention from OCD thoughts and ritualising behaviours by adopting a number of strategies, such as engaging in absorbing activities like painting and drawing. Since she loved tennis, she took this up at school and in the back garden. Akira enjoyed dancing in her room to playlists that she and her mother had made. She even devised her own strategy of singing out loud if an OCD thought popped into her mind, which she and her family thought was hilarious.

Akira learned breathing exercises and progressive muscle relaxation. She also found that formal and informal mindfulness practices helped her to focus on the 'here and now' and not to over-engage with the OCD thoughts. She was able to sit back and observe these thoughts, and gradually learn not to respond to them by checking, re-checking and ruminating. She felt that this was a huge triumph. Her anxiety was reducing, she was sleeping better, and her physical symptoms were becoming less intense. The family made sure that they acknowledged and celebrated her successes.

Help the young person to identify and challenge negative thoughts and worries. Develop alternative, more realistic thoughts and positive self-talk. Speak to them about the link between unhelpful thoughts, emotions and behaviours.

It was important to Akira to realise that her OCD thoughts were not facts, and to reduce her anxiety and belief in them. Using thought diaries, the counsellor helped Akira to identify her OCD thoughts, and to create some distance from the condition by giving it a name and seeing it as a 'glitch' or false alarm in her brain. Akira had a good sense of humour and drew a picture of her OCD 'gremlin'. This was a huge step forward.

The therapist explained that OCD 'bullies' people into believing that the obsessive thoughts are true, and compels them to perform the rituals. She told Akira that she would help her stand up to this bully and talk back to it. The way to challenge the OCD thoughts was by not performing the rituals it urges you to do. In this way, Akira could find out whether what the bully predicted was true or not. They talked about which rituals Akira felt she could try to reduce, and worked out an action plan. They began to build evidence that what the OCD predicted wasn't true, and this began to reduce Akira's anxiety.

Akira developed new and positive self-talk. She began to believe and accept that it was possible to manage her OCD. She learned to overcome the hopelessness she had felt. She would say to herself, "This is hard, but I can do it. I'm beginning to feel less worried already. I can deal with the anxiety and if I face my fears, I can beat the bully. I'm going to talk back to it. I'm becoming able to let the OCD thoughts pass and not do my checks. I want to do more and get stronger." She was clearly gaining in motivation and confidence.

Help the young person to recognise and understand any unhelpful and avoidant behaviours. Talk about helping them to reduce symptoms by gradually facing their fears and trying to get back to enjoying life.

The therapist explained to Akira and her mother that continually repeating compulsions and rituals maintains and exacerbates OCD. The person doesn't get the opportunity to learn that if they don't perform these actions, bad things do not actually happen. Even though Akira was starting to realise this, it was still difficult for her to give up her compulsive habits. Akira's mother understood the importance of helping her daughter to gradually tolerate her anxiety and reduce rituals. She could see that this was a hugely important step to defeating Akira's belief in the obsessional thoughts she was having.

How to help – Obsessive-Compulsive Disorder (OCD)

☞ Educate yourself and the child about the nature of OCD, explain to them that having OCD is not their fault, and adopt a calm, normalising and nurturing approach to tackling the problem.

☞ Talk to the child about their thoughts and feelings – if they can share what their obsessive thoughts are, and what they compel them to do, this represents a huge step forward.

☞ Seek to manage anxiety by identifying rituals that the child feels able to reduce, in order to build evidence that the catastrophic predictions of their obsessive thoughts are not correct.

☞ Investigate websites and charities and/or consider joining a parent support group – these can be a fantastic source of shared experience and advice on how best to support a child.

☞ If you feel that OCD is impacting significantly on family life, school life and/or the child's social interactions, do not attempt to manage with self-help alone but seek professional support.

☞ Begin with your GP, who can discuss the best way forward and may arrange a referral to Child and Adolescent Mental Health Services (CAMHS) or other mental health and support services.[91]

---

91 NICE (2005) *Obsessive-compulsive disorder and body dysmorphic disorder: treatment.* Available at: https://www.nice.org.uk/guidance/cg31/informationforpublic

Chapter 21: OCD-related disorders

This chapter looks at anxious behaviours that are considered to be related to Obsessive-Compulsive Disorder and commonly categorised alongside it. We will consider Trichotillomania (hair-pulling), Excoriation Disorder (skin-picking) and especially Body Dysmorphic Disorder (an obsession with perceived bodily flaws that are imagined or exaggerated). Historically, these conditions were all seen as forming part of the OCD spectrum, and *The Diagnostic and Statistical Manual of Mental Disorders* (DSM-5) classifies them as OCD-related disorders. However, in recent years experts have begun to view hair-pulling and skin-picking as more separate disorders, albeit ones that can co-occur with OCD.

> **Key Point**
>
> In recent years experts have begun to view hair-pulling and skin-picking as separate disorders, albeit ones that can co-occur with OCD.

The most appropriate self-help strategies and therapeutic treatments for all the conditions covered in this chapter are broadly similar to those used for OCD. If professional help is considered necessary, cognitive behavioural therapy (CBT) is currently considered to be one of the most effective treatments. In some cases, particularly for Body Dysmorphic Disorder (BDD), anti-depressant medications may also be prescribed to help individuals engage with therapeutic treatments.

Body-focused repetitive behaviours

Hair-pulling and skin-picking are body-focused repetitive behaviours that, along with related problems like nail-biting, affect around five per cent of the population. This repetitive self-grooming may involve picking, pulling or scraping the skin, hair or nails, which causes physical damage to the body. Whereas OCD is driven primarily by unwanted obsessions, for example with fears of bad things happening, and compulsive rituals carried out in an effort to prevent these things from coming to pass, hair-pulling and skin-picking involve repetitive behaviours that are performed to reduce tension, or even just out of habit, rather than being initiated by an unwanted intrusive thought. People feel an intense urge to pull out their hair or pick at their skin, and they experience growing tension until they do. Afterwards, they feel a sense of relief.[92]

Trichotillomania

Trichotillomania is a condition where individuals have irresistible urges to pull out hair from the scalp, eyebrows, lashes, armpits or genital areas of the body using their fingers and tweezers. This can result in bald patches and the person spending inordinate amounts of time trying to camouflage them with artificial eyelashes and eyebrows. Worrying about this causes high levels of distress. Being unable to hide these areas can lead to self-isolation, missing school and avoiding social interactions due to anxiety, low self-worth, embarrassment, shame, hopelessness and depression.[93]

Excoriation Disorder

Excoriation Disorder (sometimes called Dermatillomania) is a skin-picking condition. Individuals repetitively pick, rub, scratch or dig into their skin in order to improve its appearance. Individuals may pick at spots, freckles, moles and previous scars on their arms and face with fingernails, tweezers and even with scissors. They may also bite, squeeze or excessively rub the skin. This can result in physical pain, tissue damage and scarring.[94]

People with Excoriation Disorder can isolate themselves and spend lengthy amounts of time on their behaviours. This can cause high levels of physical pain, distress, anxiety and depression. It can impair day-to-day functioning and in particular the individuals' ability to engage in social interaction.[95]

---

92 OCD UK (2021) *Related Disorders*. Available at: https://www.ocduk.org/related-disorders/
93 OCD UK (2021) *Trichotillomania (Hair Pulling Disorder)*. Available at: https://www.ocduk.org/related-disorders/trichotillomania/
94 The TLC Foundation for Body-Focused Repetitive Behaviors (2021) *What is Excoriation (Skin Picking) Disorder?* Available at: https://www.bfrb.org/learn-about-bfrbs/skin-picking-disorder
95 OCD UK (2021) *Excoriation Disorder (skin picking disorder)*. Available at: https://www.ocduk.org/related-disorders/skin-picking/

Body Dysmorphic Disorder (BDD)

Body Dysmorphic Disorder is characterised by a distressing preoccupation with perceived defects or flaws in one's appearance, which in fact are either not visible to the outside eye or are attributable to normal human variation.[5] BDD is considered to be linked closely with OCD and the symptoms of the two conditions can be similar in that BDD involves obsessive and repetitive behaviours such as constantly checking appearance and looking in the mirror. However, there are also some important differences. In BDD, the preoccupation and compulsive behaviours are specific to the areas of the body perceived as flawed, whereas in OCD the person can have many kinds of obsessive thoughts and behaviours. Professional assessment is vital to ensure correct diagnosis and appropriate treatment, because both conditions can be present.[96]

Key facts

The prevalence of BDD in adolescents in the UK is approximately 2.2%.[97] It is a serious and debilitating disorder, and one that is associated with a high risk of suicidality.[98] As such, BDD can lead to high levels of anxiety and depression and often needs specialist clinical intervention and treatment. It can be a 'hidden condition' that is difficult to identify and often goes undiagnosed, partly because it can co-exist with other problems such as depression, OCD, social anxiety and eating disorders such as anorexia nervosa, bulimia nervosa and binge-eating. Treatment plans for BDD will take this into account, and also aim to treat any comorbid difficulties.[43]

> **Key Point**
>
> People with BDD may complain of a lack of symmetry, or feel that something is too big, too small, or out of proportion to the rest of their body.

The most common complaints seen in BDD concern the skin, nose, hair, eyes, chin, lips and overall body build. People with BDD may complain of a lack of symmetry, or feel that something is too big, too small, or out of proportion to the rest of their body. Any part of the body may be involved in BDD including the breasts or genitals. BDD

---

96   HelpGuide (2021) *Body Dysmorphic Disorder (BDD)*. Available at: https://www.helpguide.org/articles/anxiety/body-dysmorphic-disorder-bdd.htm
97   Schnackenberg, N. (2021) Young people's experiences of body dysmorphic disorder in education settings: a grounded theory. *Educational Psychology in Practice* 37:2, 202-220.
98   Veale, D., Gledhill, L.J., Christodoulou, P. & Hodsoll, J. (2016) Body dysmorphic disorder in different settings: A systematic review and estimated weighted prevalence. *Body Image* 18 168–186.

usually begins in adolescence, between the ages of sixteen and eighteen. However, milder symptoms can begin to appear from as young as twelve. It can sometimes take up to fifteen years before help is sought from mental health professionals.[99]

Causes

It is not known exactly what causes Body Dysmorphic Disorder. People may be more susceptible to developing the condition if:

- A family member has OCD, BDD or a mental health problem.
- They have experienced traumatic events such as bullying or abuse.
- They have a neurochemical imbalance.
- They have other mental health problems like an eating disorder, anxiety, depression or OCD.

In today's society, young people are exploring and forming their identities in the midst of an environment where a perfect appearance, popularity and the approval of others is commonly perceived as the route to success, happiness and fulfilment. Body image difficulties, poor self-esteem and mental health issues are increasingly linked to social media activity and appearance- and image-based apps such as Snapchat, Instagram and Facebook.[100] This has been described as an epidemic problem by mental health organisations.[101] Pressure to conform to the ideal size and body image can give rise to mental health problems such as anxiety, low mood, low self-worth, shame and a sense of failure, as young people find themselves unable to match or live up to the idealised (and often enhanced) images that they aspire to.

With that said, body image issues and a degree of self-consciousness can be a natural part of puberty and adolescent development. And encouragingly, early identification of issues can help to prevent the development of serious clinical conditions such as BDD. Psychoeducation and the use of self-help resources can be extremely effective in this regard. If a formal process of treatment is required, parents are often required to be involved and will receive support and guidance from the therapist.

---

99 Body Dysmorphic Disorder Foundation (2021) *What is Body Dysmorphic Disorder?* Available at: https://bddfoundation.org/information/what-is-bdd/

100 YMCA (2016) *It's time to Be Real about body image.* Available at: https://www.ymca.co.uk/health-and-wellbeing/feature/its-time-be-real-about-body-image

101 Mental Health Foundation (2019) *Body image: How we think and feel about our bodies.* Available at: https://www.mentalhealth.org.uk/publications/body-image-report

Behaviours and indicators to monitor

- Concern about areas including facial features, skin imperfections, body and/or facial hair, body size, shape or muscle tone, breasts and genitals.
- Experiencing extreme preoccupation and intrusive distorted thoughts and anxiety about parts of the body perceived as flawed, ugly or deformed; constantly seeking reassurance.
- Spending inordinate amounts of time comparing appearance to other people; this often takes place through social media platforms.
- Constantly checking appearance in mirrors and reflective surfaces, or avoiding looking at oneself at all; avoiding being photographed; editing pictures before posting on social media.
- Excessive grooming, and spending prolonged periods attempting to cover up, conceal or disguise features or parts of the body perceived as flawed with makeup, cosmetic treatments or loose clothing.
- Constantly seeking better ways to conceal or disguise the offending feature; spending a great deal on makeup, clothing and treatments.
- Over- or under-eating to modify body shape or weight; in extreme cases, having a desire or plan to have corrective cosmetic surgery.
- Avoiding social situations such as school, social gatherings or being in public places for fear of exposing the perceived flaw; not leaving the home unless absolutely necessary or becoming housebound.
- Self-isolation and avoidance behaviours resulting in depression, possible thoughts of self-harm and in extreme cases suicidality.

Negative ways of thinking

- Comparing and despairing: "I cannot measure up to others. They have perfect figures and looks. I'm ugly and unacceptable."
- All or nothing: "If I don't look as perfect as others then I am ugly and a total failure."
- Negative bias: "She said I look great, but only because she felt sorry for me."
- Self-criticism: "I am not good enough. I am not as good as others. I am ugly and will never be as good as I need to be. If I can only fix my horrible appearance, I will be completely happy."

How to help – Body Dysmorphic Disorder (BDD)

☞ Seek psychoeducation for yourself and your child with self-help resources. Identify the areas that they are self-conscious and worried about, and try to understand the extent of the problem. Encourage them not to measure their self-worth based on their ability to conform to unrealistic and unrelenting standards.

☞ Adopt a calm, nurturing approach. Provide a listening ear and take their concerns seriously. Show empathy and support for their emotions, and help them to identify and talk about how they are feeling. Try not to appear dismissive of their worries, as aspects of themselves that they perceive as seriously flawed may not be noticeable to you or very slight.

☞ Spend time helping them to learn and practise self-regulating and soothing techniques to manage emotions and symptoms. Adopt strategies for general wellbeing. Encourage them to develop self-kindness, acceptance and compassion, and to be less self-critical.

☞ Help them to identify the extreme self-critical negative beliefs and thoughts about themselves, and unhelpful, self-defeating behaviours that maintain and exacerbate the condition. Guide them to recognise and focus on the positive qualities and strengths they have and not to overfocus on their perceived flaws.

☞ If self-help feels inadequate, encourage them to seek help from a professional who understands and works with people with BDD. If they are unwilling, some therapists offer parent consultations and can support parents to help their children recover.

☞ Be sure to take good care for yourself; pay attention to your overall wellbeing, and accept support from family and friends.

Chapter 22: Separation anxiety

Children who become extremely worried about being apart from a parent, carer or loved one may be experiencing what is known as separation anxiety. It is thought that up to four percent of young people suffer with this as a diagnosable condition,[102] and it is the most common anxiety disorder in those under the age of twelve.[103] Separation anxiety can often be seen early in a child's life when they go to a play group or nursery and are separated from those to whom they are most attached. This is regarded as developmentally normal until around the age of two, after which point it should decline.

> **Key Point**
>
> Children who become extremely worried and distressed about being apart from a parent, carer or loved one may be experiencing separation anxiety.

Older children can also experience this kind of anxiety when they are away from the security of their loved ones, particularly if things are not going well at home or they are experiencing problems at school or elsewhere.

General features and symptoms

The common features of separation anxiety in children and young people include the following.

- Unrealistic, persistent thoughts that something bad may happen to themselves or loved ones, and that they may never see them again.
- Feeling distressed and fearful at the prospect of separation long before it happens and experiencing significant fear and distress for the entire duration of time spent away from loved ones.
- Bodily reactions to anxiety including panic attacks.

---

102 Walkup, J.T., Albano, A.M., Piacentini, J., Birmaher, B., Compton, S.N., Sherrill, J.T., Ginsburg, G.S., Rynn, M.A., McCracken, J., Waslick, B., Iyengar, S., March, J.S. & Kendall, P.C. (2008) Cognitive behavioral therapy, sertraline, or a combination in childhood anxiety. *The New England journal of medicine*, 359 (26), 2753-2766.

103 Costello, E.J., Egger, H.L. & Angold, A. (2005) The developmental epidemiology of anxiety disorders: phenomenology, prevalence, and comorbidity. *Child and adolescent psychiatric clinics of North America*, 14 (4), 631-vii.

- Nightmares about separation such as getting lost, or harm coming to themselves or loved ones; reluctance to sleep by themselves.
- Clingy behaviour and avoidance of anything which would involve separation, even for short periods of time.
- Reporting symptoms such as stomach ache, nausea or headaches to avoid having to go to school because that is probably the longest period they regularly experience separation.
- Not wanting to go on school trips, sleepovers or other social events.[19]

It can be extremely worrying to see a child in distress. Separation anxiety can be stressful and limiting for parents due to problems with being able to be apart from the young person. Parents can feel guilty about having to take the child to school or be away from home for work or other engagements. It can create disruption to family life and feel overwhelming. If the anxiety has persisted for several months and is not improving, it could be beneficial to seek an assessment from a mental health professional as the condition can continue into adulthood. This can indicate the extent of the problem and whether self-help, parental support or external intervention is necessary.

Children with separation anxiety may also have generalised anxiety, which can similarly be identified through assessment. If psychological therapy is recommended, this will usually involve helping the child with their negative thoughts and fears, relaxation training and exposure therapy. The latter exposes the child to separation in gradual steps in order to support them in getting used to feared situations and ultimately reducing the anxiety.[104]

---

104 Child Mind Institute: *What Is Separation Anxiety?* Available at: https://childmind.org/article/what-is-separation-anxiety/

Separation anxiety case study: Isabella, age 9

Isabella had begun to complain of stomach pains and feeling nauseous when it was time to leave for school and when going to friends' houses for sleepovers, which was something she had previously enjoyed. Her reluctance to be away from home had persisted for a period of about four months.

Isabella's teachers noticed that her concentration in class was deteriorating. She seemed to be distracted in lessons and had not been her usual cheerful self for some time. Isabella also began to talk about not wanting to go on a school trip which had been planned for several months and involved staying away from home for two nights. She had previously been very excited about the trip and was usually enthusiastic about any kind of school outing. Her class teacher was concerned and spoke with the pastoral head.

The school staff contacted Isabella's parents to say they were concerned that she could be experiencing anxiety. Her parents greatly appreciated their intervention and explained what had been happening at home. The school were also aware that Isabella's maternal grandmother had passed away in recent months. From discussion with her parents, they wondered whether this had been a factor in Isabella not wanting to leave her mother and if she could be struggling with separation anxiety. The school staff were very supportive and agreed to make any adjustments needed to help Isabella with getting into school and settling in class. The school counsellor agreed to speak with Isabella if it was deemed necessary.

Individual/idiosyncratic formulation: Isabella

Anxious thoughts/cognitions	Anxious emotions
■ Racing thoughts: "What if a bad thing happens to my mum when I'm at school? What if she gets ill and dies? I may never see her again." ■ "I need to be with my mum all the time to be sure she's OK." ■ "Mum has lost her mum and she is so sad. I can't cope with it." ■ "The same could happen to me now. I could lose my mum."	■ Sad and tearful ■ Apprehensive and afraid ■ Tense and unsettled ■ Panicky ■ Out of control ■ Helpless ■ Unable to concentrate ■ Lonely and isolated ■ Low mood
Physical symptoms of anxiety	Anxious behaviours
■ Shallow breathing, hyperventilation ■ Heart pounding ■ Lightheaded and dizzy ■ Shaky; hands trembling ■ Nausea; stomach ache; poor appetite ■ Tense muscles ■ Poor sleep quality; difficulty getting to sleep	■ Clingy, tearful and reluctant to leave her mother's side. ■ Avoiding sleepovers with friends. ■ Distracted and on edge in class. ■ Unable to concentrate. ■ Uncharacteristically quiet and withdrawn. ■ Frequently seeking reassurance that her mother is feeling OK. ■ Spending long periods worrying ■ Issues with school punctuality.

What helped Isabella with her separation anxiety?

Adopt and model a calm approach to the situation. Explain to the young person what you know about the problem and how it can feel, and normalise it. Identify the main issues and reasons for their worries.

Isabella's parents researched anxiety and the common challenges that are experienced by children. Her behaviour seemed to suggest that she was suffering from separation anxiety. Isabella's parents felt that her worries about being away from them could have been triggered by the loss of her beloved maternal grandmother, to whom she had been closely attached. Following this psychoeducation, they were able to approach the problem with a clearer idea of what Isabella was going through and what she might be thinking and feeling. They learned about strategies they could use to help her to deal with her feelings of loss and her separation anxiety.

Cultivate emotional awareness. Help the young person to identify and cope with their emotions. Show understanding and validate their feelings.

Isabella's parents decided that her father would talk to her about how she was feeling. This was because her mother was still at an early stage of her own grief, and it could be overwhelming for her to process the loss with Isabella. They also decided that if the situation became too stressful for them or too much for Isabella, they would seek support from the school counsellor.

Isabella's father found a book about how we can feel when someone dies to help him to talk about life cycles and loss, and he and Isabella worked through it together. There were naturally tears when Isabella talked about her feelings, but also lots of hugs and understanding. She found the book comforting as it explained the feelings she was having and normalised how bereavement is experienced. The book was placed on a shelf in the kitchen so that Isabella could look through it herself if she wished, or her parents could read it with her. This seemed to have a comforting effect, and it helped Isabella to understand and express her sadness and sense of loss.

Help the young person to learn and practise self-regulating and soothing coping strategies to manage symptoms. Adopt strategies for general wellbeing.

Isabella and her parents talked about ways to soothe and calm anxious feelings. She seemed to benefit a great deal from guided visualisations, breathing exercises and progressive muscle relaxation. Isabella was creative and loved to paint. She painted a picture of her most peaceful place and put it up on her bedroom wall. She was then able to return to that place when she felt the need by lying on her bed, focusing on the picture, evoking the peaceful feelings, and holding on to them for as long as she could. Her parents explained that it could take time to grieve for her grandmother, but that they were all in it together.

Help the young person to identify and challenge negative thoughts and worries. Develop alternative, more realistic thoughts and positive self-talk. Speak to them about the link between unhelpful thoughts, emotions and behaviours.

Isabella's father set aside some time to talk to her about negative thoughts. She had occasionally voiced what she was thinking, which provided a good place to start. Her worries were mainly around being separated from her mother, whom she had witnessed experiencing the loss of her own mother. Isabella was frightened and preoccupied with thoughts about how terribly sad and lost she would feel if the same thing happened to her. Her father told her that those kinds of worries were natural under the circumstances, but they were also unrealistic. He helped her to see that believing these thoughts was making her miserable and getting in the way of her happiness.

Isabella's father pointed out that, despite all Isabella's worrying, nothing bad had happened to her mother. The reality was that her mother was young and healthy, while Grandma was an elderly lady who had passed away due to old age. Isabella's thoughts were not facts, and what she had been worrying about was very unlikely to happen. This was a breakthrough for Isabella. She said that she felt relieved and much better having "let her scary thoughts out" and talked them through with her father. Isabella agreed to stop believing all her bad thoughts and to start realising that what she had spent so much time worrying about had not come to pass. She acknowledged that worrying was a waste of time.

Isabella was still reluctant to be away from her mother, but could see that she was missing out on lots of things she had previously enjoyed like sleepovers and her school trip.

Help the young person to recognise and understand any unhelpful and avoidant behaviours. Talk about helping them to reduce symptoms by gradually facing their fears and trying to get back to enjoying life.

Isabella remembered how much she had been looking forward to the school trip before the loss of her grandmother. She could also understand why her feelings had changed. She agreed to be brave and to try to gradually spend time away from her mother. Together they put together a hierarchy of exposure, beginning with spending short periods of time with her friends from school and gradually building up to having sleepovers again.

Isabella's parents explained that the staff at school understood how she was feeling and were happy to support her. She was very pleased about this and began to feel more confident. Isabella's parents told her that they had agreed with her teacher that she could use a signal of her choosing if she needed to go and speak to the designated pastoral lead or just spend a little time in the Quiet Room. If she was going to be late for school and needed more time to separate from her mother in the mornings, they could just let the school know and her teachers would be understanding.

Isabella told her parents that some days were harder for her than others. They arranged for her to see the school therapist once a week and she engaged well with these sessions. They met approximately six times to help her feel safe and more content in school. She then felt confident enough to reduce the sessions and have more belief in her ability to cope.

As Isabella graduated towards more social time with her friends and felt supported in school, she developed the confidence to try braver steps. Her mood improved greatly. Isabella loved to swim, and her parents ensured that she was able to do this and other physical activities to help her to continue to feel better and lower her anxiety. It was a work in progress, but things were certainly moving in a positive direction.

How to help – separation anxiety

☞ Take the time to learn about separation anxiety and identify the particular challenges the child is facing. This will give you a better understanding of what they might be experiencing and the ways in which you can offer support.

☞ Talk to the child about how they are feeling, showing empathy and understanding. Workbooks and other tools can help them understand and express what they are experiencing – see the Appendix.

☞ Help the child to find the self-soothing strategies that suit them best. Practise these together and encourage them to explore different ways of maintaining their general wellbeing, such as art or sport.

☞ Talk about the child's anxious thoughts and help them assess whether these are realistic and helpful. Help them to think about the futility of excessive worry and the impact it may be having on their life.

☞ Encourage the child to notice any avoidant behaviours that they have developed and to think about ways in which these could be tackled. Help them to gradually increase their exposure to time away from their loved ones and praise their progress.

☞ Seek the support of teachers and pastoral staff at the child's school if necessary. Their understanding can be very beneficial, and accommodations can be made for specific areas of difficulty.

Chapter 23: School anxiety and refusal

Most children and teenagers will feel some level of worry in relation to school at various times during their academic journey. However, for young people with school anxiety, the learning experience can be persistently stressful and difficult. This can reach a point where the child does not want to attend school, or is simply unable to do so. This condition of reluctance or inability to attend school due to anxiety is known as school refusal.

> **Key Point**
>
> *For young people with school anxiety, the learning experience can be persistently stressful and difficult.*

It should be noted that school anxiety can sometimes be due to one or more broader types of anxiety. These can include Generalised Anxiety Disorder (GAD) and social anxiety. For further information on these conditions please see Chapters 15 and 16 respectively.

General features and symptoms

Children and young people can feel anxiety in relation to many aspects of school life. This can include the demands of the classroom and academic performance, relationships with teachers, friendships, and bullying. Changes such as moving up to a new year group or a different school can also create difficulties, in addition to external factors such as family or health issues.

Children and young people who are experiencing school anxiety may not always confide in their parents or caregivers. It is therefore important to monitor for behaviours such as not wanting to get out of bed in the morning, complaining of illness to avoid school, truancy, uncharacteristic negative behaviour at school or at home, a decline in academic performance and engagement, or withdrawal and low mood.[105]

---

[105] YoungMinds: *School anxiety and refusal: A guide for parents*. Available at: https://www.youngminds.org.uk/parent/parents-a-z-mental-health-guide/school-anxiety-and-refusal/

School anxiety case study: Sam, age 8

Sam's school anxiety began to manifest itself during primary education. His parents were aware that he was generally quite prone to worry and did not cope well with big changes. They were concerned because an ongoing reluctance to go to school in the mornings had recently begun to escalate. He would become so distressed that they felt it was unkind and unhelpful to force him to go.

Sam's parents had spoken to his headteacher, who was supportive. Sam was offered help from the pastoral lead and school counsellor, for which his parents were very grateful. However, the primary difficulty at that point was getting Sam to actually go into school. He was halfway into his first term and they wanted to act quickly. Sam would sometimes complain of feeling nauseous and having headaches in the mornings. His mother took him to school in the car and would usually have to spend a long time preparing him to enter the building. More recently, however, Sam had been so anxious that she often had to take him home because it felt cruel to force him. This was very difficult for her, as she was a loving and protective mother. She and her husband were at a loss as to how to help their son. It was agreed with the school that they would initially seek outside support.

Sam's parents had a consultation with a therapist and agreed to go forward with treatment if Sam was willing to attend. Sam's mother went with him to the sessions to help him to engage with the treatment. Psychometric assessment indicated that Sam was struggling with generalised anxiety, and some features of social anxiety. With the help of the therapist and his mother, Sam was able to disclose the problems he was having at school. They praised him for being brave enough to share his worries. The therapist created a formulation of Sam's difficulties and began to gather information on what could be causing him to avoid going to school.

Sam told the therapist that he had a new class teacher and was worried about making mistakes and getting into trouble. This was because he had seen the teacher get angry with some boys who were particularly disruptive and disrespectful in class. The teacher had also been quite stern on a few occasions, and Sam said that he often had an angry expression on his face. Sam was a polite and cooperative boy. The therapist found that his self-esteem was much lower than average, seemingly because his self-worth was often dependent on having good relationships and the approval of others.

It is important to note that Sam had not had much time to get to know his new teacher, and was perhaps assuming the worst. He had enjoyed a supportive relationship with his previous teacher, who had always been understanding and reassuring if he struggled with tasks. The change of teacher was difficult for Sam. He was finding it hard to complete tasks in school, especially if there was a time limit. He was very worried about what might happen if he made mistakes or couldn't finish his work. He was fearful that the teacher would chastise him and make him the focus of attention. This had never actually happened, but Sam was extremely worried and focused on the possibility that it might. He predicted that if this did happen, it would be so upsetting for him that he would burst into tears in front of his class and would feel stupid and extremely embarrassed.

Sam was constantly vigilant of the teacher's facial expressions, and if he saw the slightest suggestion of a negative reaction, it would trigger his anxiety. He would become extremely worried that this was related to something he had done to displease the teacher. Furthermore, Sam was anxious that, if he felt upset, the pupils in his class would see him as 'a nervous wreck' and tease him about it. He was feeling vulnerable and anxious in school for most of the day, and ashamed that he couldn't cope. His anxiety had escalated to the point where he would struggle to get to sleep at night and worry about going to school the next day in case what he was predicting came to pass. Sam was exhausted and drained by such high levels of anxiety. He was beginning to feel very low and helpless.

Individual/idiosyncratic formulation: Sam

Anxious thoughts/cognitions	Anxious emotions
- "He looks cross. It could be something I've done wrong." - "What if the teacher is cross and it's my fault? He'll tell me off in front of the whole class. I'll cry in front of everyone. They'll think I'm stupid and tease me." - "He doesn't like me, and he'll show me up in front of everyone." - "I feel scared so something bad is going to happen." - "I won't be able to do well in school and I'll never get a good job." - "It's probably only me that can't cope. I should be able to manage and not feel this way. I'm useless." - "I shouldn't get so worried. I should be able to go to school." - "If I get one thing wrong, I've failed."	- Excessively and intensely worried most days - Mind racing with 'what ifs?' - Unsettled and apprehensive - Hypervigilant; constantly on alert - Panicky and afraid - Poor concentration - Exhausted - Alone - Unhappy and tearful
Physical symptoms of anxiety	Anxious behaviours
- Jumpy and on edge; easily startled - Breathing irregularity; hyperventilation - Heart beating fast - Dizzy - Shaky; hands trembling - Butterflies in stomach - Poor appetite - Sleep disturbance; trouble getting to sleep - Complaining of nausea and headaches	- School avoidance - Frequently seeking reassurance - High level of distress and crying - Worrying for long periods - Hypervigilant to anything going wrong - Anxious about homework and getting it all correct - Avoiding talking about worries - Checking everyone is happy and OK - Unable to relax and get to sleep at night

What helped Sam with his school anxiety?

Adopt and model a calm approach to the situation. Explain to the young person what you know about the problem and how it can feel, and normalise it. Identify the main issues and reasons for their worries.

The therapist explained the nature and symptoms of anxiety to Sam, and helped him understand that it is something natural that affects many young people. She normalised anxiety and told him that she worked with many children with similar problems. This was reassuring for Sam and his mother. They felt hopeful that he could learn how to cope with what he was feeling.

Cultivate emotional awareness. Help the young person to identify and cope with their emotions. Show understanding and validate their feelings.

Sam identified the feelings he was having with the help of mood cards. He felt relieved to have opened up and talked about what he was experiencing in the safety of the therapeutic relationship. The therapist listened, offering understanding and compassion for what Sam was going through. He was helped to avoid judging himself too severely for feeling anxious. This positive regard and understanding helped Sam to feel better about himself. With time, it also enabled him to understand how the belief in his negative unhelpful thoughts was influencing his emotions and avoidant behaviours. He felt hopeful and motivated to attend future sessions.

Help the young person to learn and practise self-regulating and soothing coping strategies to manage symptoms. Adopt strategies for general wellbeing.

Sam and the therapist worked out which coping strategies Sam felt would be most helpful to him. He practised these in the sessions and at home until he felt confident enough to employ them by himself. Sam made a list of chosen strategies that he could refer to if needed. These included:

- reaching out and talking to a trusted and understanding person
- a combined breathing and progressive muscle relaxation audio track for evenings and bedtime

- a night-time wind-down routine put in place with the help of his parents
- a relaxing guided visualisation of a peaceful place; Sam chose a tropical island
- informal mindful eating and walking
- going swimming (his favourite physical exercise) at least twice per week, and joining the swimming club at school
- getting out into the countryside on family bike rides
- doing colouring books for a sense of calm and enjoyment
- creating different playlists of songs for when he wanted to feel calm, happy or energised
- identifying his favourite healthy foods and making sure that he had plenty of these
- planning to socialise and connect more with his friends, both in and out of school

Sam's school was also keen to support him in managing his anxieties. A meeting was organised between Sam's new teacher and his parents, during which they recognised that Sam may have been misinterpreting the situation. The teacher was sympathetic, and agreed to chat with Sam to get to know him and to find out what he could do to help him to feel less anxious. The school were very understanding and – in line with recommendations from the therapist – made the following adjustments that they felt would help.

- It was agreed that the headmistress, pastoral lead and class teacher would monitor how Sam was coping when he returned to school.
- Sam was able to go back to school on a reduced timetable and was greeted in the morning by the pastoral lead before classes began. He knew her well and was happy to meet her.
- Sam was seated close to the teacher in class and away from the more boisterous pupils.
- The class teacher would ensure that Sam had clear instructions and enough time to complete tasks. He told Sam that he was happy to help him with any tasks or homework, and not to be afraid to ask.
- The class teacher was now aware of Sam's triggers and would be sensitive to these in class.
- Sam was assured that he could speak to the pastoral lead and take time out in the Quiet Room if needed. Support from the school counsellor was also available upon his return.

Help the young person to identify and challenge negative thoughts and worries. Develop alternative, more realistic thoughts and positive self-talk. Speak to them about the link between unhelpful thoughts, emotions and behaviours.

The therapist helped Sam to identify his worries and negative patterns of thinking. He was able to challenge his anxious thoughts in the following ways:

- **Negative bias:** Sam started to use a thought diary to record his feelings. This allowed him to see that he was focusing solely on the teacher's negative expressions. When Sam returned to school, the therapist encouraged him to try to notice when the teacher looked happier and when he was being supportive. Sam was asked to write this down in his thought diary as a record of evidence against the negative thoughts.
- **Personalisation:** Sam was helped to realise that he was not responsible if others were behaving badly in class and the teacher was frustrated.
- **Catastrophising:** Sam's parents had met with his teacher, who was keen to support him. Sam and the therapist agreed that based on this, the likelihood of the teacher shouting at Sam and making an example of him in class was negligible. This helped enormously in motivating Sam to get back to school.
- **Mind-reading:** Sam realised that spending time worrying about his teacher disapproving of him was futile, and that what he had been concerned about was not going to happen. It was possible that when the teacher had a seemingly negative or inscrutable facial expression, he might be preoccupied with something else and not thinking about Sam at all.
- **Emotional reasoning:** The therapist helped Sam to fact-check his thoughts and to realise that even when he did feel anxious and predict something bad would happen, it never did.
- **Fortune-telling:** Sam realised with support that he could do well in school and access the help for learning that every pupil needs. He began to believe this and felt more motivated to go to school, knowing that it was a supportive environment and that lots of significant people valued him and would help him.

- **Self-criticism/comparing and despairing:** To counter Sam's self-critical thoughts and comparison to others, the therapist talked about the nature of anxiety as a natural human response. Focusing on Sam's strengths and personal qualities helped him to develop positive self-talk and to feel better about himself: "It's not just me. Anxiety is not weird or unusual. I know now that people can be understanding and supportive and want to help me. Everyone needs help at times and that's OK."
- **Black-and-white thinking:** It was helpful for Sam to think about the natural learning process and that as part of this everyone makes mistakes. He could also see that if he didn't understand something challenging, the teacher would be happy to help.

Help the young person to recognise and understand any unhelpful and avoidant behaviours. Talk about helping them to reduce symptoms by gradually facing their fears and trying to get back to enjoying life.

Sam returned to school on a staged basis and worked gradually towards ending his therapy sessions. The measures his school had put in place enabled Sam to do this at a comfortable pace, in the knowledge that people wanted to help him. He began his phased return with hope and motivation.

Sam had learned how to manage his thoughts and feelings. He developed a good relationship with his new teacher and the pastoral lead. He was very happy to get back into a normal routine and to see his friends at school. He now knew that his anxiety could be managed, and that help was at hand if required. Sam realised that many pupils need pastoral support when they struggle with worry and difficulties in their lives. He learned that his problems were not insurmountable if he reached out to others and shared his worries, because people cared about him.

How to help – school anxiety

☞ Share what you know about anxiety with the child and help them to understand that this is something natural that affects a lot of young people. Normalise what they are feeling and offer reassurance that they will be able to overcome the challenges they are facing.

☞ Make use of resources such as mood cards to help the child to identify their feelings and share their experiences with you. Be a good listener, showing understanding and compassion for what they are going through.

☞ Help the child to explore various strategies for coping and general wellbeing that will help them to manage the symptoms of their anxiety. Practise the strategies that the child finds most helpful together until they feel confident to employ these independently.

☞ Work with the school so that teaching and support staff are aware of the specific challenges that the child is experiencing. Accommodations can be made to help the child feel less anxious and address any specific areas of concern. Support from pastoral staff or a school counsellor can also be accessed if required.

☞ Help the child to identify and challenge their negative thoughts and worries in relation to school. A thought diary can be a useful way to record and assess their feelings, and to consider alternative and more helpful ways of thinking.

☞ Talk to the child about any avoidant or unhelpful behaviours they have developed in relation to their anxiety. Work with the child and the school to explore ways to overcome these habits and support them to gradually face their worries in small manageable steps.

Part 5: Depression

Chapter 24: The teenage brain and mood difficulties

In addition to what we now know about the internal and external causes of emotional difficulties in young people, it is essential to understand that there are other forces at work during adolescence that can significantly influence mood and behaviour. Neuroscience may appear to be a complex and difficult subject,

> ## Key Point
>
> *During the adolescent years, a surge in brain development and growth can create vulnerability to negative emotions, low mood and anxiety.*

and one that is beyond most of us. However, it can be a truly fascinating area of study, especially in the context of making sense of the emotions and behaviours of our own children and young people. This chapter will provide a brief introduction to adolescent emotional and social development in the context of neuroscience. Readers seeking further insights are encouraged to refer to the titles listed in the Appendix.

During the adolescent years, a surge in brain development and growth occurs – one that can affect mental wellbeing and create vulnerability to extreme and negative emotions, low mood and anxiety. At this tender age, the multitude of pressures that young people face in general, together with the wave of emotional and neurological development that they are experiencing, can create a 'perfect storm' that may be difficult for teenagers to navigate without the understanding and guidance of the adults in their lives.

A common perception is that negativity, mood swings and volatile behaviours among teenagers are mainly attributable to fluctuations in the sex hormones oestrogen, progesterone and testosterone. However, the reality is not quite that simple. Research shows that low mood and erratic emotions can also be due to the natural but turbulent processes involved in the development of the adolescent brain.[106]

Mental health problems can often begin during the teenage years. At this time of significant neurological and physical development, adolescents are grappling with social and emotional changes and can be particularly vulnerable to stress and difficulties such as anxiety and

---

[106] Siegel, D.J. & Bryson, T.P. (2012) *The Whole-Brain Child*. New York, NY: Random House.

depression.[107] The Young Minds mental health charity states that at present approximately eighty thousand children and young people in the UK are suffering from depression,[108] and according to the Child Mind Institute's 2017 *Children's Mental Health Report*, most mental health problems begin before the age of twenty-four.[109]

Adolescence is a critical period for young people, and intervention in the first year of depression and suicidality is crucial. Parental understanding of teenage brain development and support from parents and carers can help to prevent or mitigate lifelong mental health struggles. The school environment can also have a significant effect. The above report found evidence that the provision of education about adolescent mental health and anti-stigma programmes improved attitudes to mental health by 68%, as well as boosting treatment-seeking behaviour and outcomes.

Dr Andrew Garner, an expert on early brain development and the effects of stress and trauma, emphasises how important it is for parents and carers to be vigilant regarding signs of emotional problems in children and young people, even if they are not directly related to neurological development. Dealing with pressure and stress is no small challenge for a fully mature brain, much less one that is in transition from childhood to adulthood and from concrete to abstract thinking, and all teenagers exhibit at least occasional outbursts or episodes of misjudgement. But, Garner argues, if teenagers are withdrawn, acting out, not eating or sleeping regularly, or they are letting their grades or dreams pass them by, then it is time for parents to sound the alarm and seek help.[29]

Expert View

"As long as teenagers are social, eating and sleeping well, and working toward the fulfilment of their plan, their parents should be happy."

Andrew Garner

Stages of neurological development

The brain develops in stages and reaches its full size in adolescence; in girls this is around age eleven, and in boys around age fourteen. This heralds the most significant surge of brain growth and cognitive

---

107 National Institute of Mental Health (2020) *The Teen Brain: 7 Things to Know*. Available at: https://www.nimh.nih.gov/health/publications/the-teen-brain-7-things-to-know

108 YoungMinds *Depression: Your guide to depression and finding the help and support you need*. Available at: https://www.youngminds.org.uk/media/xl2nf0df/young-minds-depression.pdf

109 Child Mind Institute (2017). *2017 Children's Mental Health Report*. Available at: https://childmind.org/awareness-campaigns/childrens-mental-health-report/2017-childrens-mental-health-report/

development since infancy. It has been described by neuroscientists as a period of neural 'pruning' when the fully-grown brain begins to organise and tidy up neural pathways or connections. As learning takes place during the adolescent years, new neural pathways are created and old connections dissipate. This carries on into adulthood, until individuals reach their mid-twenties.

Two key parts of the brain are the *amygdala* and the *pre-frontal cortex*. The amygdala is often referred to as the instinctive, emotional part of the brain, while the pre-frontal cortex enables logic, decision-making, problem-solving, abstract thought, impulse control and emotional regulation. It is important to be aware that the pre-frontal cortex is the final part of the brain to mature in a person's mid-twenties, and that prior to this the amygdala has a significant influence on emotions and behaviours. This helps to explain adolescent mood swings, poor concentration, and impulsive irrational behaviours which can seem devoid of awareness or the ability to think through consequences. Put simply, teenagers are frequently in a highly reactive 'flight-or-fight' mode, governed by their amygdala.

When fully developed, the pre-frontal cortex enables us to 'read' the emotions of other people more accurately. Before this has occurred, however, teenagers can often negatively misinterpret the emotions and motives of others and respond inappropriately. The key thing to remember is that in adolescence the logical areas of the brain are not yet fully mature, and the cognitive and emotional regulation skills are underdeveloped. Consequently, teenagers can struggle with interpersonal relationships. They can be vulnerable, irrational, volatile and easily upset. They can also behave in unreasonable and hurtful ways towards other people in their lives.[110]

During the neural pruning process, teenage behaviour can be changeable and confounding for those around them. This is a time when they are likely to challenge boundaries and engage in impulsive and unhelpful behaviours. Such actions can be unfathomable, exhausting and worrying for parents and carers at home, and also for teachers in the school setting. We often see young people reacting first and thinking later or exhibiting extreme frustration and negativity. Neuroscientists have carried out brain imaging studies that provide high quality, tangible evidence of brain development in the teenage years. They argue that adolescent brain immaturity can explain much of the behaviour we see. It can be

---

110 Norfolk and Waveney Children & Young People's Health Services (2021) *Teenage Brain*. Available at: https://www.justonenorfolk.nhs.uk/childhood-development-additional-needs/supporting-development/teenage-brain

illuminating and reassuring for parents to understand how the teenage brain can be in such disarray, and it can explain to some extent the extreme, changeable and upsetting moods and behaviours that we may witness in our sons and daughters.

Importantly, it can also be hugely beneficial for teenagers themselves to understand the stages of brain development that they are going through. It can help them to make sense of the turmoil they may be experiencing – why they feel emotions so intensely, why they often think in negative ways and why they may struggle with low moods. Simply explaining this to young people and offering understanding can provide them with significant relief.

From a positive and hopeful perspective, the developing teenage brain has the ability to learn and change; a quality known as neuroplasticity. Young people's ability to adapt and respond to their environment offers parents, carers and educators the opportunity to guide them in healthy directions and establish more helpful neural pathways. According to the National Institute of Mental Health in the United States, engaging in exercise, creative pursuits and challenging academic or mental activities promotes and aids learning and maturity in the adolescent brain. Mindfulness-based practice can also help teenagers cope with stress and low mood. The teenage brain is resilient and, in spite of vulnerability at this stage of development. Given the correct environment and conditions for growth the majority of individuals emerge as healthy, functional adults.

How to help – understanding teenage brain development

According to the New Zealand website KidsHealth,[111] some key points to know and remember about adolescent brain development and its effects on teenagers are as follows:

☞ A safe environment where teenagers have consistent loving support is vital for the brain to develop well.

☞ Adults who talk to children as they are growing up really help.

☞ When talking to teenagers, be careful to check what emotion they are seeing in you, and make sure you acknowledge their emotions first and help them think about what they are feeling.

☞ Young people need adults to believe in them and encourage them.

☞ Teenagers respond better to rewards than to punishment.

☞ Young people need clear, consistent boundaries, and it is very important that their growing capacity and ability to do things independently is respected.

---

111 KidsHealth (2021) *Adolescent Brain Development*. Available at: https://www.kidshealth.org.nz/adolescent-brain-development

Chapter 25: Depression and low mood

Depression is a common mental health problem that affects more than a quarter of a billion people across the world.[112] It can be experienced by individuals of any age, nationality or socio-economic status. It occurs in around one to three percent of children and young people – mainly older adolescents, but also younger children. On a more reassuring note, depression is among the most treatable of emotional disorders and, while it is naturally a big worry for parents if they suspect that their child may be experiencing problems, evidence suggests that more than three quarters of all young people who receive help go on to feel better and enjoy greatly improved wellbeing.[113] Identification, prevention and early intervention are the keys to avoiding low mood escalating to clinical levels.

> **Key Point**
>
> *More than three quarters of all young people who receive help for low mood go on to feel better and enjoy greatly improved wellbeing.*

It was once believed that clinical depression occurred only in adults, and that teenage low mood was just a normal part of 'growing up'. However, studies in the 1970s and 1980s showed that depression can occur well before adulthood. Since then, there has been significant research into depression in children and young people, with a recent focus on early identification and evidence-based clinical and self-help treatments.[114]

Of course, the journey of adolescence remains a turbulent one, and short-term low mood can be a normal occurrence. In addition, concerns have recently grown about the impact of lockdowns, social distancing, isolation and educational disruption on the mental health and development of young people. A study found that depression in young people increased

---

112 World Health Organization (2021) Depression. Available at: https://www.who.int/health-topics/depression#tab=tab_1
113 Action Mental Health (2021) Depression in young people – recognising the signs and knowing where to get help. Available at: https://www.amh.org.uk/news/depression-in-young-people/
114 Verduyn, C., Rogers, J. & Wood, A. (2009) Depression: Cognitive behaviour therapy with children and young people. Routledge.

during the first COVID-19 UK lockdown, and more so than anxiety.[115] It can therefore be confusing for parents and carers to understand whether what they are seeing is simply typical teenage behaviour, or whether there is cause for more concern. If you are worried or in doubt, a consultation with a mental health professional can help.

General features and symptoms

We are not completely sure what causes children and young people to suffer depression, or why some young people experience it while others do not. In teenagers, depression is more common among girls than boys, and low self-worth can be a significant factor. For the general population, depression can be due to genetics, early life experiences, or a complex combination of social, biological and psychological factors. Major adverse life events like bereavement, relationship problems, health issues, anxiety and stress seem to be causal factors.[116] Some individuals have one episode of depression and recover, but the illness is more easily triggered in those who have had it before. Some people struggle throughout their lives, and a small percentage experience depression psychosis (distressing thoughts, or hearing voices) or bipolar disorder (extreme low and high mood). These are more severe problems, and usually require clinical intervention. [117]

There are various theoretical models that offer explanations of depression. Cognitive and behavioural models will be used here. From a cognitive perspective, Beck identified three mechanisms responsible for depression.[118] This is referred to as the Negative Triad of Depression, and it involves automatic negative thoughts and feelings about three areas:

1. Ourselves
2. Other people and the world in general
3. The future

---

[115] Bignardi, G., Dalmaijer, E.S., Anwyl-Irvine, A.L., Smith, T.A., Siugzdaite, R., Uh, S. & Astle, D.E. (2020) Longitudinal increases in childhood depression symptoms during the COVID-19 lockdown. *Archives of disease in childhood*, 106(8), 791–797.

[116] British Medical Journal Best Practice (2021) *Depression in children*. Available at: https://bestpractice.bmj.com/topics/en-gb/785

[117] Royal College of Psychiatrists (2021) *Depression in children and young people: for young people*. Available at: https://www.rcpsych.ac.uk/mental-health/parents-and-young-people/young-people/depression-in-children-and-young-people-for-young-people

[118] Beck, A.T. (1967) *Depression: Causes and treatment*. University of Pennsylvania Press.

Depression can build up gradually and may not be apparent to begin with. As it develops, thoughts, emotions and behaviours become increasingly more negative and intense. Negative emotions, thinking and rumination can cause us to behave in unhelpful ways; for example, depressed people tend to withdraw from others and to socialise less. They become isolated and, as this continues, their mood worsens. They can also lack energy, have trouble concentrating or feeling motivated, have poor quality of sleep and changes in appetite, and struggle to do things they once enjoyed.

Sadness is a natural response to things that are stressful or distressing. However, when such feelings last for a long time and young people find it hard to contain them, they can become overwhelmed and feel hopeless. High levels of despondency and depression can lead to significant problems at home, in school, with relationships and in daily functioning. Young people may stop attending school, engage in substance misuse, form inappropriate relationships or begin to think about harming themselves. The risk of dangerous behaviours like these is a key reason why the earliest possible detection and treatment of depression is vital.

How to help – common signs of depression in young people

If you are concerned that a young person may be struggling with depression, these are some useful areas to monitor:[119]

☞ **Lethargy**
- Lack of interest in life
- Low energy; exhausted and drained
- Loss of enthusiasm for things they used to enjoy
- Loss of libido
- Becoming withdrawn and avoiding others

☞ **Negativity**
- Prolonged low mood
- Feeling sad and gloomy most days
- Self-critical
- Low self-worth
- Thoughts about suicide or self-harm

☞ **Volatility**
- Irritable and easily agitated
- Tearful and easily distressed
- Difficulty making decisions and concentrating
- Not coping with things that used to be easy to deal with
- Avoiding taking part in unusual activities

☞ **Physical problems**
- Sleep disturbance
- Overeating and weight gain
- Poor appetite and weight loss
- Mentioning aches and pains
- Menstrual cycle disruption
- Alcohol or substance misuse

---

[119] NHS Child and Adolescent Mental Health Services (2021) *Depression / Low mood*. Available at: https://camhs.elft.nhs.uk/Conditions/Depression--Low-mood

Deconstructing depression

Depression is easier to understand if broken into separate elements such as thoughts, emotions, physical symptoms and behaviours. All these areas are interrelated, and each contributes to the negative cycle of low mood. Below is a generic representation of what depressed people may think and feel, the symptoms they may experience and the ways in which they may behave.

Depressive thoughts/ cognitions	Depressive emotions
■ Negative bias towards self.	■ Sad
■ Catastrophising, predicting worst outcomes: "It will be unbearable. I can't cope. It will just get worse."	■ Pessimistic
	■ Helpless
	■ Sense of failure
■ Mind-reading: "Everyone thinks I'm boring and grumpy."	■ Loss of pleasure and enjoyment
	■ Guilty
■ Self-criticism: "I'm useless and pathetic."	■ Worthless
	■ Hopeless and despairing
■ Thoughts of suicide or self-harm: "I hate myself. I can't go on."	■ Suicidal
	■ Self-loathing
■ Dwelling on past mistakes.	■ Easily moved to tears
■ Black-and-white thinking with no middle ground: "I'm a failure."	■ Empty/numb
	■ Indecisive
■ Shoulds and musts; comparing and despairing: "I shouldn't feel so low"; "Others cope, but not me."	■ Lethargic
	■ Drained
	■ Irritable
■ Discounting positive things: "My friends want to meet up, but only because they feel sorry for me."	■ Restless
	■ Poor concentration
	■ Alone, isolated and cut-off
■ Generalising: If one thing doesn't go well, nothing else will.	
■ Fortune-telling, pessimism re the future; "Things won't get better."	
■ Hopeless and helpless view of self and situation; loss of confidence.	

Physical symptoms of depression	Depressive behaviours
<ul><li>Fatigue</li><li>Poor energy levels</li><li>Appetite disturbance; eating less or more than usual</li><li>Weight change</li><li>Tension in the muscles, bodily aches</li><li>Poor sleep quality; sleeping more or less than usual</li><li>Restless or agitated</li><li>Headaches, stomach aches, or aches in the arms or legs (these somatic/physical symptoms are common in children)</li></ul>	<ul><li>Unexplained crying or sadness</li><li>Low motivation to do anything</li><li>Loss of usual energy levels</li><li>Procrastination</li><li>Unable to make small decisions</li><li>Unable to concentrate</li><li>Academic performance deteriorating</li><li>Social withdrawal and cutting themselves off from family and friends</li><li>Anhedonia – loss of interest and inability to feel pleasure doing things they usually enjoy</li><li>Spending long periods alone, worrying and ruminating</li><li>Uncharacteristic irritability and frustrated behaviour</li><li>School avoidance and refusal</li><li>Over or undereating</li><li>Sleeping too much or too little compared to usual</li><li>Complaining of aches and pains with no obvious cause</li></ul>

Depression case study: Maya, age 14

Maya's parents were concerned about changes in their daughter's mood and behaviour. The family had moved house four months earlier because her father had found a new job. It was a huge change for Maya because their new home was in a different area, and she had changed school. She had left behind a group of good friends and was struggling to adjust. Her form teacher reported that she seemed quiet and withdrawn and hadn't joined any friendship groups. She felt that Maya was not fully engaged socially or in her school work despite a good academic record. She had previously been sporty, but she had shown no interest in activities in the new school.

Maya's mother was worried as Maya increasingly seemed to want to avoid speaking to her parents and appeared angry and resentful. She began retreating to her room as soon as she came back from school and staying there for long periods. She always seemed to be in a low and irritable mood. Her appetite had decreased and, if she was asked to eat more, she would get angry and frustrated. It was difficult to get her up for school in the mornings, and sometimes she would say that she felt unwell and couldn't go in.

Maya's mood had not improved over time as her parents hoped it would. They had tried to give her space, but she seemed increasingly withdrawn and was constantly miserable. When her parents went into her room, she would be lying on the bed sleeping or staring into space with the blinds closed. They told her that they were worried, but she would tell them to leave her alone and slam the door. At one point, she screamed that she couldn't stand her life. This frightened them. Maya then burst into tears, and finally confided that she felt she couldn't cope, that nobody cared about her and that she was worried that she would never make good friends again. She also missed her wider family, who now lived far away.

Maya's parents reassured her that they loved her dearly and were very worried about her. They discussed how a combination of help from them and talking therapy could support her in managing her feelings, and Maya eventually agreed to give it a try. Her mother praised her for opening up and pointed out that the changes she had experienced would be hard for anyone to cope with. Maya acknowledged that her parents did understand what she was going through and wanted to help.

Maya's mother contacted their GP, who suggested talking therapy. The waiting list was lengthy, and the doctor suggested that they seek help as soon as possible. They contacted an accredited practitioner via a counselling and psychotherapy regulatory body website,[120] and had an initial consultation with the therapist. Maya then began to attend sessions. She agreed to her parents' involvement at times when the therapist felt it was appropriate. The therapist carried out an assessment which indicated that Maya was experiencing symptoms of anxiety and low mood.

---

120 BABCP: The online CBT Register for the UK and Ireland: https://www.cbtregisteruk.com/

Individual/idiosyncratic formulation: Maya

Depressive thoughts/cognitions	Depressive emotions
■ Self-critical: "I'm weird and nobody likes me. I'm a useless mess." ■ Negative view of others: "Even my parents don't care; nobody loves me." ■ Catastrophising: "I'll never make new friends. My old friends will forget me. It will never get better." ■ Mind-reading: "They think I'm weird and don't want to be friends. There's no point trying." ■ Fortune-telling, predicting that things will never get better. ■ Hopeless and helpless, no hope of being able to feel any better. ■ Loss of confidence: "I can't stand feeling like this. It's getting worse. I don't want to carry on."	■ Irritable ■ Sad most days ■ Lethargic ■ Drained ■ Despairing ■ Hopeless ■ Pessimistic ■ Alone and isolated ■ Loss of pleasure and enjoyment ■ Easily moved to tears ■ Feeling empty/numb at times ■ Worthless; poor self-esteem ■ Thoughts of being better off if no longer alive; no intent or plan ■ Alone, isolated and cut off ■ Anxious about being at school and around her peers
Physical symptoms of depression	Depressive behaviours
■ Fatigue ■ Poor energy levels ■ Appetite disturbance; eating less than usual ■ Poor sleep quality; sleeping more than usual ■ Restless ■ Anxiety and panic symptoms before and during school ■ Tummy aches, headaches	■ Ceasing contact with previous friends and extended family ■ Avoiding contact with pupils at new school ■ No eye contact or conversation ■ Staying in background and keeping quiet to avoid attention ■ Withdrawing/self-isolating ■ Interacting with family only when necessary ■ Refusing to talk about it ■ Spending time alone ruminating and focusing on negatives ■ Stopping physical activity and sports ■ Refusing to go on family outings

What helped Maya with her depression?

Adopt and model a calm approach to the situation. Explain to the young person what you know about the problem and how it can feel and normalise it. Identify the main issues and reasons for their worries.

Maya met with the therapist to complete the assessment. She and her mother then attended the first therapy session. The therapist explained that Maya was experiencing a combination of anxiety and depression symptoms. She helped Maya to understand that what she was experiencing was a natural response to loss and coping with such big changes in her life. She told Maya that she was brave to seek help. This helped to normalise Maya's experiences, and to reassure her that she could recover.

Cultivate emotional awareness. Help the young person to identify and cope with their emotions. Show understanding and validate their feelings.

Maya had several one-to-one sessions with the therapist to enable her to express her feelings about all aspects of her life. She needed a safe, private space to do so, particularly in light of her conflicting emotions towards her parents. The therapist explained to Maya and her mother that this could be a difficult stage, and that unconditional compassion and support outside sessions, without discussion of the sessions' content, would be helpful. Maya was courageous, and in time managed to approach and share her feelings. The therapist gave Maya's mother a website link about how to support teenagers with low mood.[121]

Help the young person to learn and practise self-regulating and soothing coping strategies to manage symptoms. Adopt strategies for general wellbeing.

During therapy, Maya learned various ways to manage her symptoms. She and the therapist practised a range of strategies, including breathing training, progressive muscle relaxation, guided visualisation exercises and mindfulness. Maya chose an app for her phone that contained a

---

[121] Child Mind Institute: *What to Do if You Think Your Teenager Is Depressed.* Available at: https://childmind.org/article/how-to-help-your-depressed-teenager

range of exercises and allowed her to practise and use the strategies outside the sessions. Maya's parents, after consulting with the therapist, encouraged and supported her to try yoga and aromatherapy, to re-establish contact with friends and family, to resume things that she had previously enjoyed, to interact with her school mates and to consider taking up sports again. They let her choose nutritious foods for family meals, and her appetite returned. Through this process, Maya's mood improved, and she began to accept the love and nurturing connection that she had previously enjoyed with her parents.

Help the young person to identify and challenge negative thoughts and worries. Develop alternative, more realistic thoughts and positive self-talk. Speak to them about the link between unhelpful thoughts, emotions and behaviours.

The therapist helped Maya to identify and talk about her negative thoughts and worries. Together, they explored more balanced and realistic ways of thinking to help with the low mood, and to challenge her anxious thoughts and pessimism. They also worked on monitoring Maya's unhelpful feelings using thought diaries, which enabled them to discuss what Maya had recorded in order to build evidence against her unrealistic and unhelpful ways of thinking and gain perspective. Maya and the therapist also worked on her self-esteem by focusing on her positive qualities and strengths. From these sessions, they developed several positive self-talk affirmations. For example: "I am loved and cared for." "I have good friends and I can make new ones." "I can overcome this if I am kind to myself." "It's OK to get help." "I will get better."

Help the young person to recognise and understand any unhelpful and avoidant behaviours. Talk about helping them to reduce symptoms by gradually facing their fears and trying to get back to enjoying life.

The therapist helped Maya to identify her goals and take small steps to re-engage with important people in her life. Maya recognised that feeling so low had perhaps prevented her from making any effort to make friends. They began by supporting Maya to contact her grandmother, to spend more time with her parents doing enjoyable activities, to message the old friend she missed most and to become more active.

Maya said that there was one girl in school who had been kind, and she agreed to try to connect with her. The school supported her – the pastoral lead said he understood that she was having a difficult time, and he would help in any way he could. He offered to identify pupils who might make good friends for Maya and encouraged her to consider resuming netball.

The process had begun, and over time Maya began to feel better; she was engaging more and her mood improved. The support of her parents, school staff and the therapist helped her to re-engage with friends and family. She began to realise that she had people who loved and cared for her, and her self-esteem improved. She learned that the best way to cope with feeling low was not to withdraw, but to reach out to trusted people and to talk about her feelings. She began gradually to interact with other pupils and to make new friends.

Chapter 26: Specific strategies for depression

Sensing that a child may have depression can be a very worrying and emotional time for parents and carers. You may feel powerless, anxious, sad, guilty or responsible in some way for the child's suffering. When someone is depressed and withdrawn, they can often feel flat, drained and gloomy. As a result, it's not easy for them to connect with family and friends or to reach out and talk to others about how they are feeling. Yet, if a child you care for is suffering with low mood or depression, your understanding and support can be a hugely significant factor in helping them to recover.

> *Key Point*
>
> *If a child you care for is suffering with low mood or depression, your support can be a hugely significant factor in helping them to recover.*

It is difficult to approach someone you love who is withdrawn and feeling down. You may anticipate an angry or indignant response, which could be upsetting for everyone, and this can make it hard to know where to begin. However, gentle consistency and persistence can help young people to reach out. Valuable advice can be found on the HelpGuide website.[122] Be sure to also look after yourself, and to maintain your own wellbeing and emotional resilience – this is vital to enable you to support your child.

Steps for supporting young people with depression

Listen and engage

The starting point for communicating with a depressed young person in a supportive and helpful way is to listen calmly and compassionately, and to acknowledge how they are feeling about their lives, even if this does not reflect your own view of the reality of their situation. Try not to question or reason with their concerns and worries; just listen. Give them space if that's what's needed; however, be consistent in communicating that you care and want to help in whatever way

---

[122] HelpGuide: *Parent's Guide to Teen Depression:* Available at: https://www.helpguide.org/articles/depression/parents-guide-to-teen-depression.htm

they choose. Tell them that you love them, and that you're concerned because you've noticed they seem to be feeling down. Instil hope and tell them you're there for them, that they are not alone, and that you'll help them get whatever help they need.

They may be feeling hopeless, so it's important to help them understand that depression is not abnormal, and it can go away if they accept help and support. It may be helpful to gently find out if something has happened that has caused them to feel this way. If your child is unwilling to open up to you, they may nevertheless see the benefit in talking to someone else who is not involved in their daily lives, such as a counsellor. If so, support them in making contact, remembering appointments and getting to sessions.

Understand and notice unhelpful behaviours

Learning all you can about depression and coming to understand and recognise the unhelpful coping behaviours that could be contributing to the maintenance of your child's low mood, is a very important step. Helping the child to begin to change these unhelpful coping strategies, and to adopt more positive and healthy behaviours, can be essential to their recovery. Encourage them to reach out and rekindle uplifting connections with caring and supportive friends and relatives and help them to take gradual steps towards socialising again. An evidence-based technique called 'behavioural activation' involves tackling low mood by increasing activity levels in a manner that is realistic and achievable, and a useful guide to this is available from the Australian Centre for Clinical Interventions.[123]

Regulate sleep and eating

Irregular sleeping habits can often develop if someone has depression. They may sleep too much, or more than usual. Helping them to establish a night-time wind-down routine and good sleep hygiene can help enormously with low mood, energy levels and day-to-day functioning. The Centre for Clinical Interventions has produced some helpful information and worksheets that may help you to begin to work on problem areas.[124]

---

123 Centre for Clinical Interventions: *Back from the Bluez: Behavioural Strategies for Managing Depression.* Available at: https://www.cci.health.wa.gov.au/-/media/CCI/Consumer-Modules/Back-from-The-Bluez/Back-from-the-Bluez---02---Behavioural-Strategies.pdf

124 Centre for Clinical Interventions: *Sleep.* Available at: https://www.cci.health.wa.gov.au/Resources/Looking-After-Yourself/Sleep

A depressed young person's appetite can also alter. They may eat too little or too much, and junk foods tend to be a favourite. Disturbance in food intake or a poor diet can have a huge impact on energy levels, functioning and mood stability, so agree to have regular meals and healthy snacks to maintain energy, and prepare meals that are rich in nutrients, vitamins and Omega-3 fatty acids. Complex carbohydrates can boost serotonin levels and sustain energy. Avoid consuming too much sugar, refined carbohydrates, trans fats, saturated fats, and foods with high levels of preservatives.

Encourage exercise and physical activity

Physical activity can produce positive neurochemicals in the brain and naturally boost mood. Exercise can lift energy levels and have similar effects to antidepressant medication. Encourage the young person to resume exercise and sporting activities that they once enjoyed, or help them to find new ones that they feel they would enjoy. This can take time, and at first it may not feel as good as it once did, but be patient.

Work with the young person to develop a list of wellbeing activities that can help them relax and lift their mood. They can refer to this when required, rather than trying to come up with something on the spot when they feel flat and unmotivated. The table below offers some ideas:

How to help – improving mood through wellbeing activities and strategies

When drawing up a list of wellbeing activities and strategies, it's good to have a balance of physical activities and calming, relaxing ones. It can be helpful to ask the young person to rate the activities in terms of improved mood. Encourage them to do more of the most effective ones and keep developing the list and noticing what makes them feel happy.

- Enjoy the sunshine: sunlight boosts vitamin D production, which improves mood and can generate a sense of wellbeing.

- Get out and about: walking, going for a run, going to the gym or going to the beach can all help to alleviate stress and anxiety.

- Make mood playlists: one for energy, dancing and feeling upbeat, and another with soothing and calming music for quieter times.

- Read a favourite book, draw, paint or do some craft work.

- Contact a friend by calling, video-chatting or messaging, or arrange to meet up with friends or family in person.

- Have a pamper evening, with special occasion luxuries.

- Stroke a beloved family pet, or practise yoga and mindfulness meditations to help with mood and energy levels.

Social media and depression

A poll for the Young Minds Matter series, which was supported by the Duchess of Cambridge, found that over 80% of parents felt that social media exposure made young people more prone to emotional difficulties. Research conducted by Sei Yon Sohn and colleagues found evidence that excessive use of smartphones was associated with increased vulnerability to poor mental health in one in four children, and called for more research to determine boundaries between helpful and harmful levels of technology usage.[125] Dr Michelle O'Reilly of the University of Leicester has argued that, as part of treatment, mental health practitioners need to ensure that they assess the influence of social media on anxious or depressed young people.[126]

> **Expert View**
>
> "We often hear from young people about the devastating effects of online bullying, and about how easy it is to find distressing content."
>
> Tom Madders, Young Minds

Psychologist and broadcaster Dr Linda Papadopoulos says that recent research on the effects of social media on the mental health of young people suggests that excessive users of social media are three times more likely to be depressed than occasional users.[127] Also, those who use social media for more than two hours a day are more likely to have fair or poor mental health than occasional users. This is due to three main factors:

1. The impact of social media on sleep
2. Using it as a comparison tool (comparing and despairing)
3. Chasing likes on social media and becoming dependent on these to generate self-worth and boost self-esteem

---

125 Sohn, S., Rees, P., Wildridge, B., Kalk, N. & Carter, B. (2019). Prevalence of problematic smartphone usage and associated mental health outcomes amongst children and young people: systematic review, meta-analysis, and GRADE of the evidence. *BMC Psychiatry* 19 356.

126 O'Reilly, M. (2020) Social media and adolescent mental health: the good, the bad and the ugly. *Journal of Mental Health* 29:2, 200-206.

127 Papadopoulos, L. (2017) *How does social media impact the mental health of young people?* Available at: https://www.internetmatters.org/hub/expert-opinion/social-media-impact-mental-health-young-people/

According to Tom Madders, Campaigns Director at Young Minds, young people are, surprisingly, not always conscious that the pressures of social media can be causing them anxiety. Whilst social media has its benefits, parents must be vigilant and monitor the use of these platforms. Schools too can play a vital role in promoting digital resilience by offering compulsory lessons on how to use social media safely. Spending time on social media has been shown to increase the risk of exposure to bullying and trolling; the National Bullying helpline offers support and guidance to parents and schools on cyberbullying and mental health.[128]

When to seek professional help

As we have seen, it can be hard for parents, carers and schools to know whether a young person is experiencing serious problems with low mood or just going through temporary tough times. Individuals experience low mood differently, and they display different symptoms as a result.

In general, there is cause for concern if:

- Low mood is frequently preventing a child or young person from enjoying home or school life
- It is affecting their usual day-to-day functioning and is significantly impacting on their emotional wellbeing.
- The low mood and negativity are prolonged, and self-help has not worked sufficiently to alleviate the difficulties.
- The young person is showing a lack of enjoyment and motivation to do things that they used to enjoy.
- Avoidance and withdrawal are significant.

If your son or daughter, or a child you care for, is having thoughts about not wanting to go on with life, then this is a clear sign that they need help and should be acted on immediately. Contact your GP or local mental health crisis team. If you need immediate help, stay with the child and contact the NHS helpline for your region. They provide support and guidance on a 24-hour basis, and you can speak to a mental health professional who will be able to talk you through what to do in the moment and arrange for assessment or treatment if necessary. A list of helplines and other resources both for general support and for times of emergency can be found in the Appendix.

---

128 National Bullying Helpline: *Cyberbullying and online harassment advice*. Available at: https://www.nationalbullyinghelpline.co.uk/cyberbullying.html

Part 6: Conclusion

Chapter 27: Summary

This chapter recaps on the myriad ways in which we can help our children and young people to learn how to manage the symptoms and challenges of anxiety and depression. With the increasing prevalence of mental health problems in people of all ages, the importance and benefits of parents, carers, teachers and other adults being able to recognise and identify children and young people suffering with emotional difficulties cannot be overstated. This is particularly important in the aftermath of the COVID-19 pandemic.

> **Key Point**
>
> *The importance and benefits of adults being able to recognise children and young people suffering with emotional difficulties cannot be overstated.*

It is important to realise and keep in mind from the outset that anxiety and depression are common mental health problems: They are often natural and understandable responses to life events. Both are highly treatable, early intervention and prevention are vital to minimise the risk of an individual developing more serious or persistent conditions.

Begin with psychoeducation

If we are to understand what our children and young people could be experiencing, we need to know about the key characteristics of the various types of anxiety and depression. Psychoeducation about the causes of mental health problems can help us to understand individual symptoms and presentations. This enables parents, carers and teachers to recognise warning signs, and to identify mental health problems at home and in school in order to ensure early intervention and prevention. It is not uncommon for anxiety and depression to coexist, and a combination of symptoms and behaviours from both conditions can be present.

Create the best possible conditions and environments for children and young people

Children and young people need environments that help them to feel secure and enhance their social and emotional development. Yet parents, carers and teachers have many responsibilities and priorities to balance. Providing a secure base for our children and young people – and letting them know that we care and are there to support them – is the starting point for the emotional healing and recovery process. It is often not easy for children and young people to open up and talk about how they are feeling, and if they experience difficulties it can feel safer to withdraw and internalise their emotional problems. Being consistently and emotionally available for them is key.

Listen to young people

Parents and educators can find it hard to know where to start in providing an environment that encourages high levels of wellbeing among young people, or how to begin to help a child in need. It seems essential to know what our children and young people themselves feel is important in helping them to thrive and to feel happy and content. The ONS conducted a valuable survey that asked young people what they considered important to their wellbeing and good mental health, and allowed them to tell us what they feel are the most positive conditions for healthy growth and development.

> ## Key Point
> *Positive and healthy relationships, safe spaces and activities, support for health and wellbeing, and having basic needs met are the principal factors that young people identify as being key to a happy life.*

Positive and healthy relationships, safe spaces and activities, support for health and wellbeing, and having basic needs met are the principal factors that the young people identified as being key to a happy life. Stability, secure attachment, and feeling consistently cared for, protected and safe in the world are their most key basic needs. These are clearly protective factors and pre-requisites for happiness, contentment, and positive and healthy emotional and social development. With these needs met, children and young people will be empowered and enabled to function well in the world.

Early intervention and teamwork are essential

Early intervention, prevention and the promotion of mental health awareness are key to managing all forms of anxiety and depression. When parents, teachers and mental health professionals work together as a team around a child or young person struggling with mental health conditions, this can help enormously in achieving positive outcomes. It reassures them and gives them hope and a sense of being supported and in good hands.

A staged approach to intervention

When approaching the task of helping a young person who is struggling with worry or low mood, we have recommended a staged approach throughout the relevant chapters of this book, as follows:

1. Adopt and model a calm approach to the situation. Explain to the young person what you know about the problem and how it can feel, and normalise it. Identify the main issues and reasons for their worries.
2. Cultivate emotional awareness. Help the young person to identify and cope with their emotions. Show understanding and validate their feelings.
3. Help the young person to learn and practise self-regulating and soothing coping strategies to manage symptoms. Adopt strategies for general wellbeing.
4. Help the young person to identify and challenge negative thoughts and worries. Develop alternative, more realistic thoughts and positive self-talk. Explain the links between unhelpful thoughts, emotions and behaviours.
5. Help the young person to recognise and understand any unhelpful and avoidant behaviours. Talk about helping them to reduce symptoms by gradually facing their fears and trying to get back to enjoying life.

Provide a range of evidence-based strategies to help with emotional difficulties

Part 2 of this book contains a comprehensive range of evidence-based coping strategies and techniques to help to alleviate anxiety and low mood. The strategies presented include diaphragmatic deep breathing, progressive muscle relaxation, guided visualisations and mindfulness meditations. It is also important to pay attention to good sleep, eating and physical self-care, as well as to make time for relaxation, enjoyment and emotional self-care.

When you have read the chapter on anxiety or depression that is most relevant to the young person in your care, go to the Appendix. This provides a useful range of self-help resources in the form of links to websites to mental health organisations, and to materials for parents and schools to use.

Know what to do at times of extreme distress

It is important to know what to do in case of emergency in order to keep a young person safe. If an individual's difficulties escalate and they lose self-control, the priority is to manage the situation until the crisis has passed and calm is restored. Try to stay calm and composed yourself, and speak to the young person in a soothing, comforting tone. Talk about something else to distract them from their symptoms, and show them how to regulate their breathing to feel calmer. Each young person will have their own additional coping strategies that they prefer, and when the storm has passed and they are thinking clearly it is a good idea to encourage them to make a list of strategies that they find effective and can call on in times of need.

Challenge unhelpful thoughts

If you are helping a young person to cope with emotional difficulties, encourage them to express their worries and challenge unhelpful ways of thinking. Negative thinking patterns can convince us that things are much worse than they really are, and if we are struggling with anxiety or low mood then it is easy to have absolute belief in them. However, in reality these thoughts are not necessarily supported by any actual evidence. They can and should be reality-checked and challenged if they are not an accurate reflection of what is happening in the real world.

Identify avoidant behaviour

Anxious children will often stay away from anything that might trigger their anxiety, which to some extent seems logical enough. However, this method of coping is both unhelpful and ineffective because it provides only short-term relief. In the longer term, it will actually serve to prolong the anxiety. By constantly avoiding potentially stressful situations, the young person never has the opportunity to test their predictions about how bad these situations will really be, and whether or not they will cope. It is important to help anxious or depressed children to reduce avoidance.

From home to school

Within the educational context, a consistent and supportive relationship between teachers and their pupils is thought to be a key factor in helping young people to feel secure and engage well in the learning process. Knowledge of attachment theory in the school environment could help teachers to understand unusual or concerning behaviours, and reduce the risk of misinterpreting insecure, anxious or depressed presentations as disruptive or defiant. There are also specialist mental health organisations that offer information and guidance to help educational professionals implement a whole-school approach to mental health and wellbeing.

In the classroom

It may not be obvious that a pupil is struggling with anxiety or low mood if they internalise their difficulties and are well-behaved in the classroom. To mitigate the risk of overlooking young people who may be struggling, there are considerations that educational staff can bear in mind – and strategies that can be used to support a young person who may be in need of help. Classroom layout, break times, managing change, dealing with absence, and the approach taken to potentially stressful events like class presentations and tests will all have an impact on a young person's wellbeing at school.

Share real-life case studies

Parts 3-5 of this book contain real-life case presentations of young people with different forms of anxiety and depression, and describe the strategies that were used in each case by parents, carers, teachers and schools. The detailed accounts of how various interventions were applied to individuals in real-life situations aim to offer guidance on how children and young people have been helped and how you can adopt these strategies to support your own children and young people in addressing their difficulties and moving on with their lives in a positive, forward-looking way.

Reach out for help when necessary

Awareness and psychoeducation regarding the mental health difficulties that children and young people may experience can enable us to detect problems and to consider whether self-help is sufficient and appropriate. However, parents and teachers are not mental health professionals, so it's important to reach out for support from experienced specialists when necessary to ensure the best and most appropriate interventions. Even at this most difficult of times, knowing that you will do whatever it takes to help will be a comforting and positive message for the child or young person.

Compassionate quotations

The following compassionate quotations have always stood out to me as poignant reflections of how difficult and, at the same time, how courageous it is if young people do manage to reach out and share their feelings with us. They are shared here to instil hope and empowerment.

> *"And the day came when the risk to remain tight in a bud was more painful than the risk it took to blossom."*
> Anaïs Nin

> *"Self-care is how you take your power back."*
> Lalah Delia

> *"My dark days made me strong. Or maybe I already was strong, and they made me prove it."*
> Emery Lord

Chapter 28: A last word to parents and carers

Children and young people can find it very difficult to understand what is happening to them when they feel anxious or low, and this can be frightening and distressing for them. They often don't know how to cope with difficult emotions or what to do, and they become so overwhelmed that they are unable to begin to tell you what is wrong. As a result, you may initially interpret any changes in your child's behaviour as them being difficult, rather than realising that this is borne out of emotional turmoil.

> **Key Point**
>
> *Young people often don't know how to cope with difficult emotions, and they become so overwhelmed that they are unable to tell you what is wrong.*

Noticing the early warning signs that your son or daughter is anxious or feeling low is key. And if you find yourself in this position, talking with them and showing understanding and compassion can make a huge difference for you both. Acknowledging their worries and taking them seriously is very important, even if from your perspective those worries may seem exaggerated or unwarranted. Doing so can ensure the earliest possible intervention and prevent the development of more serious problems.

It is very helpful to assure children and young people that they are not at the mercy of difficult emotions – they can learn how to deal with them. Make the most of times when they are not experiencing periods of anxiety or depression Teach them how to practise self-soothing calming and relaxation skills that can be employed in moments of need. Learning and practising these coping strategies with your child can be beneficial for you too.

Being a parent can be highly fulfilling and rewarding, but it isn't always easy. Supporting your son or daughter when they are unhappy or in distress can be very difficult and emotionally challenging for parents. This is a time to look after yourself too. It is important to step back and not feel responsible or that you are not a good parent. Have a trusted person you can talk to, and draw upon sources of support, such as friends and family, to allow you some time for yourself. It is important to make time to relax and do things you enjoy.

It can be hugely beneficial for children and young people to feel that they have support both at home and in school, so contact your child's teacher, headteacher, head of year or school counsellor to let them know that there are difficulties and ask for support. If things become overwhelming, reach out for specialist help. Remember, the purpose of the experts you may be referred to is not to judge you but to support you in helping the young person you care for to recover. Asking for help is a sign of strength, and by reaching out you are clearly demonstrating your love and concern.

It is an incredibly positive and helpful step for anyone working with young people to take proactive steps to gain greater general mental health awareness. It is also beneficial to learn about the various types of anxiety and depression, in addition to the factors that can trigger these distressing but common conditions. Equipped with this knowledge, we are more likely to notice early warning signs and respond in a timely and appropriate way.

The purpose of this book is to convey an encouraging and optimistic message that anxiety and depression are natural, understandable and treatable human conditions. I hope that it will serve to normalise experiences, offer reassurance, and instil the confidence and courage to seek a light at the end of the tunnel.

Chapter 29: A last word to teachers and schools

My experience of working with school referrals and school staff over the years has been truly positive, uplifting and encouraging. Headteachers, teachers, teaching assistants, and pastoral care and guidance staff have shown a high level of care and support to their pupils with mental health difficulties, and a growing commitment to providing compassionate, inclusive, and supportive school environments – in other words, the best environments for children and young people in terms of fostering positive mental health and learning.

> **Key Point**
>
> *My experience of working with school referrals and school staff over the years has been truly positive, uplifting and encouraging.*

In the past, people of all ages with mental health problems were too often subjected to unfair discrimination and poor treatment. An open, inclusive, normalising and destigmatising culture in society and schools around mental health problems will encourage young people who may be in distress and quietly suffering to understand that support is available, and that it's a good thing to ask for help. If schools can provide a supportive, nurturing and secure environment for pupils to learn, this is ideal for their development.

Schools are working hard to ensure that the mental health needs of children and young people are identified and met consistently. However, whilst Government initiatives are being rolled out successfully in some parts of the country, this is not happening quickly enough to meet the needs of schools and communities in other regions. It is important that such deficits in provision continue to be addressed and resolved, in order to ensure that adequate levels of support to help children and young people with mental health difficulties are available to all schools, parents and communities.

It is recognised that many schools have made great progress in the incorporation of ideas and approaches from attachment theory within the educational setting. Knowledge of attachment theory in the context of school could help teachers to understand unusual and concerning behaviours of pupils, and reduce the risk of misinterpreting insecure, anxious or depressed behaviours as disruptive or defiant. In my experience, many schools already have pastoral provision in these areas and continually strive to make improvements for the children and young people under their care.

While teachers can and should be aware of and vigilant against possible mental health issues among their pupils, they cannot be expected to be experts. Therefore, they should be provided with clear referral guidelines and appropriate contact details for specialists. There is also a need for schools and parents to be provided with adequate resources to support young people at home and at school if onward referral is not considered necessary – for example, to be provided with appropriate and adequate self-help resources and links to supportive mental health organisations.

For young people experiencing a challenging period in their lives, having clear, consistent support at school as well as at home is an essential foundation for recovery. Now and into the future, our focus must be on escalating support to schools, parents, colleges and communities to help those individuals among our children and young people who are suffering from anxiety, depression or any other form of mental health difficulty.

Index of *How to Help* advice

First aid in times of extreme anxiety or panic 35
Talking about feelings 41
Diaphragmatic deep breathing 45
Progressive muscle relaxation 46
Visualising a safe and happy place 47
Establishing good sleep habits 50
Regulating eating problems 52
Relaxing activities 56
Mindfulness practices 58
Challenging unhelpful thoughts 66
Overcoming avoidant behaviours 71
Supporting children and young people in school 76
In the classroom 82
When to seek professional support 90
Generalised anxiety 99
Social anxiety 109
Panic attacks 119
Specific phobias 129
Post-Traumatic Stress Disorder (PTSD) 141
Obsessive-Compulsive Disorder (OCD) 152
Body Dysmorphic Disorder (BDD) 158
Separation anxiety 166
School anxiety 175
Understanding teenage brain development 183
Common signs of depression in young people 188
Improving mood through wellbeing activities and strategies 200

Appendix

Further reading and other sources of information

Chapter 2: Prevalence and provision

- *Mental Health of Children and Young People in England, 2020.* Wave 1 follow up to the 2017 survey: https://files.digital.nhs.uk/CB/C41981/mhcyp_2020_rep.pdf
- *Coronavirus: Impact on Young People with Mental Health Needs:* https://www.youngminds.org.uk/media/esifqn3z/youngminds-coronavirus-report-jan-2021.pdf
- *Life on Hold: Children's Well-being and Covid-19:* https://www.childrenssociety.org.uk/information/professionals/resources/life-on-hold

Chapter 3: Causes and consequences

- https://www.verywellmind.com/what-is-attachment-theory-2795337
- https://incredibleyears.com/programs/iy-online/

Chapter 4: Identifying problems

- **Children and young people's views**
  - https://www.ons.gov.uk/peoplepopulationandcommunity/well-being/articles/childrensviewsonwellbeingandwhatmakesahappylifeuk2020/2020-10-02
- **Identifying mental health problems**
  - https://www.nhs.uk/mental-health/feelings-symptoms-behaviours/feelings-and-symptoms/anxiety-disorder-signs/
  - https://www.nhs.uk/mental-health/children-and-young-adults/advice-for-parents/children-depressed-signs/

- **Challenges for parents and school staff**
  - https://www2.ed.gov/parents/academic/help/adolescence/adolescence.pdf
  - https://www.mindmate.org.uk/im-a-parent-or-carer/parenting-teenagers/
  - https://incredibleyears.com/programs/iy-online/.
  - *Mental health problems in people with learning disabilities: prevention, assessment, and management*: https://www.nice.org.uk/guidance/ng54

Chapter 5: Where to begin

- **Looking after yourself**
  - https://www.youngminds.org.uk/parent/survival-guide/

Chapter 6: Talking about difficult feelings

- **Psychoeducation**
  - https://youngminds.org.uk/find-help/for-parents/parents-guide-to-support-a-z/parents-guide-to-support-anxiety/#what-is-anxiety
  - https://childmind.org/article/what-to-do-and-not-do-when-children-are-anxious/
  - https://www.youngminds.org.uk/parent/a-z-guide/depression-and-low-mood/https://childmind.org/topics/depression-mood-disorders/

- **Emotional awareness**
  - https://www.justonenorfolk.nhs.uk/emotional-health/children-young-peoples-emotional-health/emotional-health-activities/feelings-activities
  - https://www.justonenorfolk.nhs.uk/childhood-development-additional-needs/talk-play/older-children-and-teens

- **Mood cards**
  - Harrn A (2021) *The Mood Cards: Make Sense of Your Moods and Emotions for Clarity, Confidence and Well-being*. London: Welbeck Publishing Group.
  - Chateez mood cards: https://chateez.co.uk/

- **Apps**
  - https://www.camhs-resources.co.uk/apps-1

Chapter 7: Strategies for soothing and self-regulation

- **Diaphragmatic deep breathing**
  - https://www.cci.health.wa.gov.au/-/media/CCI/Mental-Health-Professionals/Anxiety/Anxiety---Information-Sheets/Anxiety-Information-Sheet---08---Breathing-Retraining.pdf
  - https://www.anxietycanada.com/articles/calm-breathing-how-to-do-it/
  - GoZen breathing exercise: www.youtube.com/watch?v = Uxbdx-SeOOo

- **Progressive muscle relaxation**
  - https://www.cci.health.wa.gov.au/-/media/CCI/Mental-Health-Professionals/Panic/Panic---Information-Sheets/Panic-Information-Sheet---05---Progressive-Muscle-Relaxation.pdf
  - GoZen progressive muscle relaxation exercise: https://www.youtube.com/watch?v = cDKyRpW-Yuc

- **Guided visualisations**
  - https://relaxkids.com/
  - www.youtube.com/playlist?list = PL8snGkhBF7njO0QvtE97AJFL3xZYQSGh5
  - www.greenchildmagazine.com/guided-relaxation/
  - https://www.moodcafe.co.uk/media/26930/Relaxleaflet.pdf
  - Kerr C (2005) *Enchanted Meditations for Kids*. Sevenoaks: Diviniti Publishing
  - Kerr C (2007) *Rays of Calm: Meditations for Teenagers*. Sevenoaks: Diviniti Publishing

- **Mindfulness**
  - https://mindfulnessinschools.org/wp-content/uploads/2013/02/MiSP-Research-Summary-2012.pdf
  - https://www.derbyshire.gov.uk/site-elements/documents/pdf/social-health/children-and-families/mental-health-and-wellbeing/emotional-and-mental-health-toolkit.pdf
  - https://wellbeingforkidsuk.com/
  - www.youtube.com/playlist?list = PL8snGkhBF7ngDp1oJtx5VcjwatxZn8xLK
  - www.youtube.com/watch?v = DWOHcGF1Tmc

- Smiling Mind app for mindfulness: www.smilingmind.com.au/smiling-mind-ap
- Saltzman A (2016) *A Still Quiet Place for Teens: A Mindfulness Workbook to Ease Stress and Difficult Emotions*. Oakland: New Harbinger Publications.

Chapter 8: Sleeping, eating and physical self-care

- **Get active**
  - https://www.getselfhelp.co.uk/docs/BACES.pdf
  - Hutt RL (2019) *Feeling Better: CBT Workbook for Teens: Essential Skills and Activities to Help You Manage Moods, Boost Self-Esteem, and Conquer Anxiety*. San Antonio: Althea Press.

- **Get enough sleep**
  - https://www.cci.health.wa.gov.au/Resources/Looking-After-Yourself/Sleep
  - Huebner D (2008) *What to Do When You Dread Your Bed: A Kid's Guide to Overcoming Problems With Sleep*. Washington, D.C: Magination Press.

- **Regulate eating problems**
  - https://www.mentalhealth.org.uk/sites/default/files/food-for-thought-mental-health-nutrition-briefing-march-2017.pdf
  - https://www.icanotes.com/2018/04/04/10-foods-that-boost-mental-health/

Chapter 9: Relaxation, enjoyment and emotional self-care

- **Relaxing and absorbing activities**
  - https://www.annafreud.org/on-my-mind/self-care/

- **Feeling a sense of achievement**
  - Weekly motivator sheet: https://static1.squarespace.com/static/5e5736c87fe0d104c7787dbb/t/6069f3bdcd509969f5f734e3/1617556415828/WEEKLY + MOTIVATOR.pdf
  - Weekly activity diary: https://www.get.gg/docs/BACEdiary-weekly.pdf

Chapter 10: Challenging unhelpful thoughts

- https://www.getselfhelp.co.uk/docs/UnhelpfulThinkingHabitsWithAlternatives.pdf

- **Worry Time and Worry Jar exercises**
  - Worry Time: https://www.cci.health.wa.gov.au/~/media/CCI/Mental-Health-Professionals/Generalised-Anxiety/Generalised-Anxiety---Information-Sheets/Generalised-Anxiety-Information-Sheet---05---Postpone-your-Worry.pdf
  - Worry Jar: https://www.comfortinganxiouschildren.com/putting-worries-box-jar-calms-anxious-kids/

- **Thought diaries**
  - Paul Stallard's workbook is a useful resource for thought challenging and developing alternative thoughts with young people: Stallard, P. (2018) *Think Good, Feel Good: A Cognitive Behavioural Therapy Workbook for Children and Young People, 2e.* Chichester Wiley.
  - Barnardos have devised an online programme for identifying negative thoughts. Working through with this with nine- to 17-year-olds or asking them to access the Pesky Gnats programme can be a good way to start the process: https://www.barnardos.org.uk/ready-player-b/pesky-gnats
  - https://static1.squarespace.com/static/533eb028e4b0ba34df9be688/t/57cdd56abebafb56981251e1/1473107306390/Cognitive+Distortions+For+Teens.pdf
  - https://www.therapistaid.com/therapy-worksheet/worry-explorationquestions/cbt/adolescents
  - https://www.getselfhelp.co.uk/docs/ThoughtRecordSheet7.pdf
  - https://www.getselfhelp.co.uk/docs/MoodDiary.pdf
  - https://www.therapistaid.com/therapy-worksheets/cbt/adolescents

- **Mental health apps**
  - https://www.camhs-resources.co.uk/apps-1

- **Journaling**
  - https://www.independent.co.uk/extras/indybest/kids/books/best-kids-journal-child-gratitude-happy-b1821016.html

- **Positive self-talk and compassion**
  - https://positivepsychology.com/positive-self-talk/
  - https://tools.positivepsychology.com/self-compassion-pack

Chapter 11: Recognising avoidant behaviours

- https://www.anxietycanada.com/sites/default/files/FacingFears_Exposure.pdf
- https://childmind.org/article/what-to-do-and-not-do-when-children-are-anxious/

Chapter 12: The school culture and environment

- https://www.mentallyhealthyschools.org.uk/whole-school-approach/
- Make it Count campaign: https://www.mentalhealth.org.uk/campaigns/mental-health-schools-make-it-count-scotland
- https://www.mentalhealth.org.uk/publications/make-it-count-guide-for-pupils
- https://www.mentalhealth.org.uk/publications/make-it-count-guide-for-parents-and-carers
- https://www.mentalhealth.org.uk/publications/make-it-count-guide-for-teachers
- **General strategies for school staff**
    - https://www.sec-ed.co.uk/best-practice/managing-anxiety-in-the-classroom-mental-health-wellbeing-pastoral-students-teenagers-teachers-schools
    - https://www.sec-ed.co.uk/best-practice/anxiety-and-depression-co-morbidity-mental-health-wellbeing-students-schools/

Chapter 13: In the classroom

- https://classroom.kidshealth.org/classroom/index.jsp?Grade = 0&Section = welcome

Chapter 14: Types of anxiety and when to seek help

- https://www.nhsinform.scot/illnesses-and-conditions/mental-health/anxiety-disorders-in children
- https://kidshealth.org/en/parents/anxiety-disorders.html
- https://youngminds.org.uk/find-help/for-parents/parents-guide-to-support-a-z/parents-guide-to-support-anxiety/

- **Self-help resources**
  - https://www.nhsinform.scot/illnesses-and-conditions/mental-health/mental-health-self-help-guides/anxiety-self-help-guide
  - https://www.rcpsych.ac.uk/mental-health/parents-and-young-people/information-for-parents-and-carers/worries-and-anxieties---helping-children-to-cope-for-parents-and-carers
  - https://youngminds.org.uk/find-help/for-parents/parents-guide-to-support-a-z/parents-guide-to-support-anxiety/
  - www.worrywisekids.org/
  - www.childrenwithanxiety.com/

- **The fight, flight or freeze response**
  - https://www.health.harvard.edu/staying-healthy/understanding-the-stress-response
  - https://www.nytimes.com/2017/10/26/well/live/fear-anxiety-therapy.html

- **When to seek professional help**
  - https://www.youngminds.org.uk/young-person/your-guide-to-support/guide-to-camhs/#WhatisCAMHS
  - https://www.mind.org.uk/media/7089/anxiety-and-panic-attacks-2021-pdf-version.pdf
  - https://childmind.org/article/should-i-get-care-for-my-child/

Chapter 15: General anxiety

- **Self-help guides**
  - https://www.youngminds.org.uk/parent/a-z-guide/anxiety/
  - http://www.selfhelpguides.ntw.nhs.uk/devon/leaflets/selfhelp/Anxiety.pdf
  - https://www.helpguide.org/articles/anxiety/generalized-anxiety-disorder-gad.htm
  - https://www.happyconfident.com/shop/online-courses/?gclid = CjwKCAjwiY6MBhBqEiwARFSCPu2PLJy7ZJRtBveG6teUHwtJc8uiGOgnm39ddRtOP79NvC6jWZ7IKRoCSAwQAvD_BwE&utm_source = google&utm_medium = cpc&utm_content = Anxiety + Classes + For + Kids&utm_campaign = emotions + courses + for + children + - + search + - + broad + - + UK + - + ROAS

- **Books**
  - Creswell C & Willetts L (2007) *Overcoming Your Child's Shyness and Social Anxiety: A Self-Help Guide Using Cognitive Behavioral Techniques*. Constable & Robinson, London.
  - Josephs, S. A., & Overdrive Inc. (2017) *Helping Your Anxious Teen: Positive Parenting Strategies to Help Your Teen Beat Anxiety, Stress, and Worry*. Oakland: New Harbinger Publications.
  - Huebner D & Matthews B (2009) *What to Do When You Worry Too Much: A Kid's Guide to Overcoming Anxiety*. Washington, D.C: Magination Press.
  - Huebner D & Morris RC (2003) *Sometimes I Worry Too Much, But Now I Know How to Stop: A Book to Help Children Who Worry When They Don't Need To*. Plainview, N.Y: Childswork/Childsplay.
  - Huebner D & McHale K (2020) *Something Bad Happened: A Kid's Guide to Coping with Events in the News*. London: Jessica Kingsley Publishers.

Chapter 16: Social anxiety

- **Self-help guides**
  - https://www.nhsinform.scot/illnesses-and-conditions/mental-health/mental-health-self-help-guides/social-anxiety-self-help-guide (NHS Inform, 2020)
  - https://www.helpguide.org/articles/anxiety/social-anxiety-disorder.htm
  - https://www.verywellmind.com/social-anxiety-disorder-in-children-3024430
  - http://www.selfhelpguides.ntw.nhs.uk/devon/leaflets/selfhelp/Shyness%20and%20Social%20Anxiety.pdf
- **Books**
  - Creswell C & Willetts L (2007) *Overcoming Your Child's Shyness and Social Anxiety: A Self-Help Guide Using Cognitive Behavioral Techniques*. Constable & Robinson, London.
  - Walker BF & Tompkins MA (2021) *Social Anxiety Relief for Teens: A Step-By-Step CBT Guide to Feel Confident and Comfortable in Any Situation*. Oakland: New Harbinger Publications.

Chapter 17: Panic and agoraphobia

- **Self-help guides**
  - https://www.youngminds.org.uk/young-person/my-feelings/panic-attacks/#Howtohelpsomeonewhoishavingapanicattack
  - https://www.helpguide.org/articles/anxiety/panic-attacks-and-panic-disorders.htm
  - https://www.hpft-iapt.nhs.uk/sites/default/files/2020-12/Coping%20with%20Panic.pdf
  - https://www.cci.health.wa.gov.au/Resources/Looking-After-Yourself/Panic

- **Books**
  - Collins-Donnelly K (2013) *Starving the Anxiety Gremlin: A Cognitive Behavioural Therapy Workbook on Anxiety Management for Young People.* London: Jessica Kingsley Publishers.
  - Collins-Donnelly K (2014) *Starving the anxiety gremlin for children aged 5-9: A cognitive behavioural therapy workbook on anxiety management.* London: Jessica Kingsley Publishers.
  - Shannon J & Shannon D (2015) *Anxiety Survival Guide for Teens: CBT Skills to Overcome Fear, Worry and Panic.* Oakland: New Harbinger Publications.

Chapter 18: Specific phobias

- **Self-help guides**
  - https://www.nhs.uk/mental-health/conditions/phobias/overview/
  - https://www.mind.org.uk/information-support/types-of-mental-health-problems/phobias/types-of-phobia/
  - https://www.anxietycanada.com/sites/default/files/adult_hmspecific.pdf

- **Books**
  - Bourne EJ (1995) *The Anxiety and Phobia Workbook, Second Edition.* Oakland: New Harbinger Publications
  - Creswell C & Willetts L (2007) *Overcoming Your Child's Shyness and Social Anxiety: A Self-Help Guide Using Cognitive Behavioral Techniques.* Constable & Robinson, London.

- Chansky TE & Stern P (2014) *Freeing Your Child from Anxiety: Practical Strategies to Overcome Fears, Worries, and Phobias and Be Prepared for Life--From Toddlers to Teens.* New York: Harmony.

Chapter 19: Trauma-related anxiety

- **Self-help guides**
    - https://www.youngminds.org.uk/young-person/mental-health-conditions/ptsd/
    - https://childmind.org/guide/helping-children-cope-after-a-traumatic-event/
    - https://www.helpguide.org/articles/ptsd-trauma/helping-children-cope-with-traumatic-stress.htm

- **Books**
    - De Thierry B (2017) *The Simple Guide to Child Trauma: What It Is And How to Help.* London: Jessica Kingsley Publishers.
    - Creswell C & Willetts L (2007) *Overcoming Your Child's Shyness and Social Anxiety: A Self-Help Guide Using Cognitive Behavioral Techniques.* Constable & Robinson, London.
    - Stallard P (2018) *Think Good, Feel Good: A Cognitive Behavioural Therapy Workbook for Children and Young People, Second Edition.* Chichester: Wiley
    - Smith P, Perrin S, Yule W & Clark DM (2010). *Post-Traumatic Stress Disorder: Cognitive Therapy with Children and Young People.* London: Routledge.

Chapter 20: Obsessive-Compulsive Disorder (OCD)

- **Self-help guides**
    - https://www.anxietyuk.org.uk/wp-content/uploads/2020/10/Helpling-your-child-with-Obsessive-Compulsive-Disorder.pdf
    - https://www.clinical-partners.co.uk/insights-and-news/child-and-adolescent-services/item/what-causes-ocd-in-children-and-adolescents
    - https://childmind.org/guide/quick-guide-to-obsessive-compulsive-disorder-ocd/

- https://www.ocduk.org/ocd/types/
- https://peaceofmind.com/education/types-of-ocd/magical-thinking/
- https://www.youngminds.org.uk/young-person/mental-health-conditions/ocd/#WhatisOCD

- **Books**
  - **For children:**
    - Huebner D & Matthews B (2015) *What to Do When Your Brain Gets Stuck: A Kid's Guide to Overcoming OCD*. Washington, D.C: Magination Press
  - **For young people / teens:**
    - Benton CM & March JS (2006) *Talking Back to OCD: The Program That Helps Kids and Teens Say, "No Way" -- and Parents Say, "Way to Go"*. United States: Guilford Publications.
    - Huebner D & McHale K (2018) *Outsmarting Worry: An Older Kid's Guide to Managing Anxiety*. London: Jessica Kingsley Publishers.
  - **OCD UK recommends a number of books:**
    - Challacombe F, Oldfield VB & Salkovskis PM (2011) *Break free from OCD*. London: Vermilion.
    - Fitzgerald S (2015) *The Beating OCD Workbook: Teach Yourself*. United Kingdom: John Murray Press.
    - Veale D & Willson R (2005) *Overcoming obsessive compulsive disorder: A self-help guide using cognitive behavioral techniques*. London: Robinson.

Chapter 21: OCD-related disorders

- **Trichotillomania: Self-help guides**
  - https://www.ocduk.org/related-disorders/trichotillomania/
  - https://www.nhs.uk/mental-health/conditions/trichotillomania/
  - https://www.bfrb.org/learn-about-bfrbs
  - https://www.bfrb.org/learn-about-bfrbs/trichotillomania
  - https://www.bfrb.org/index.php?option = com_content&view = article&id = 40&Itemid = 28

- Self-help strategies: https://www.bfrb.org/component/taxonomy/term/list/20/42
- Resources: https://www.bfrb.org/learn-about-bfrbs/articles-videos/term/list/13

- **Trichotillomania: Books**
  - Mansueto CS (2021) *Overcoming Body-Focused Repetitive Behaviors for Good.* New Harbinger Publications.
  - Keuthen NJ, Stein DJ & Christenson GA (2001) *Help for hair pullers: Understanding and coping with trichotillomania.*
  - Golomb RG & Vavrichek SM (2000) *The hair pulling "habit" and you: How to solve the trichotillomania puzzle.* Silver Spring, Maryland: Writers' Cooperative of Greater Washington.
  - Penzel F (2003) *The Hair-pulling Problem: A Complete Guide to Trichotillomania.* New York: Oxford University Press.
  - Salazar C (2005) *What's happening to my child?: A guide for parents of hair pullers.* Sacramento, Ca: Rophe Press.

- **Excoriation Disorder / Dermatillomania: Self-help guides**
  - https://www.ocduk.org/related-disorders/skin-picking/
  - https://www.nhs.uk/mental-health/conditions/skin-picking-disorder/
  - https://www.bfrb.org/learn-about-bfrbs
  - https://www.bfrb.org/learn-about-bfrbs/skin-picking-disorder
  - https://www.bfrb.org/index.php?option=com_content&view=article&id=40&Itemid=28
  - Self-help strategies: https://www.bfrb.org/component/taxonomy/term/list/20/42
  - Resources: https://www.bfrb.org/learn-about-bfrbs/articles-videos/term/list/13

- **Excoriation Disorder / Dermatillomania: Books**
  - Mansueto CS (2021) *Overcoming Body-Focused Repetitive Behaviors for Good.* New Harbinger Publications.
  - Stratton M (2018) *Stop Picking on Me: Make Peace With Yourself and Heal Nervous Habitual Obsessive Compulsive Skin Picking.* (n.p.): CreateSpace Independent Publishing Platform.
  - Pasternak A & Fletcher T (2014) *Skin picking: The freedom to finally stop.*

- Pasternak A. (n.d.) *Skin Picking: The Freedom We Found* (n.p.): Annette Pasternak.
- Huebner D & Matthews B (2009). *What to do when bad habits take hold: A kid's guide to overcoming nail biting and more.* Washington, D.C: Magination Press.

■ **Body Dysmorphic Disorder (BDD): Self-help guides**
- https://www.ocduk.org/related-disorders/bdd/
- https://www.nhs.uk/mental-health/conditions/body-dysmorphia/
- https://bddfoundation.org/information/
- https://bddfoundation.org/information/what-is-bdd/
- https://bddfoundation.org/support/support-in-the-uk/nhs-services-for-bdd/
- Support groups in the UK: https://bddfoundation.org/support/support-groups-in-the-uk/
- Podcast: https://bddfoundation.org/podcast-beating-bdd/
- https://bddfoundation.org/wp-content/uploads/2021/04/Young-peoples-experiences-of-body-dysmorphic-disorder-in-education-settings-a-grounded-theory-Schnackenberg-MARCH-2021-1-1.pdf
- https://www.helpguide.org/articles/anxiety/body-dysmorphic-disorder-bdd.htm

■ **Body Dysmorphic Disorder (BDD): Books**
- Morgan N (2019) *Body brilliant: A Teenage Guide to a Positive Body Image*. London: Franklin Watts.
- Veale D, Clarke A, Willson R (2013) *Overcoming Body Image Problems Including Body Dysmorphic Disorder: A Self-Help Guide Using Cognitive Behavioral Techniques* (Large Print 16pt). Australia: ReadHowYouWant.com, Limited.
- Callaghan L (2020) *Body Image Problems & Body Dysmorphic Disorder: The definitive treatment and recovery approach*. Newark: Trigger Publishing.
- Wilhelm, S (2006) *Feeling good about the way you look: A program for overcoming body image problems*. New York: Guilford Press.
- Cash TF (2008) *The Body Image Workbook: An Eight-step Program for Learning to Like Your Looks (A New Harbinger Self-help Workbook)*. New Harbinger Publications, Inc.
- Phillips KA (2009) *Understanding Body Dysmorphic Disorder*. United Kingdom: Oxford University Press, USA.

- Phillips KA (2005) *The Broken Mirror: Understanding and Treating Body Dysmorphic Disorder.* United Kingdom: Oxford University Press.
- Neziroglu FA, Khemlani-Petal S & Santos MT (2012) *Overcoming body dysmorphic disorder: A cognitive behavioral approach to reclaiming your life.* Oakland, CA: New Harbinger Publications.
- Pope HG, Olivardia R & Phillips KA (2000) *The Adonis complex: How to identify, treat, and prevent body obsession in men and boys.* New York: Free Press.

Chapter 22: Separation anxiety

- **Self-help guides**
    - https://www.helpguide.org/articles/anxiety/separation-anxiety-and-separation-anxiety-disorder.htm
    - https://childmind.org/article/what-is-separation-anxiety/
    - https://www.anxietycanada.com/disorders/separation-anxiety-2/
- **Books**
    - Creswell C & Willetts L (2007) *Overcoming Your Child's Shyness and Social Anxiety: A Self-Help Guide Using Cognitive Behavioral Techniques.* Constable & Robinson, London.
    - Children and bereavement: https://shop.winstonswish.org/collections/books

Chapter 23: School anxiety and refusal

- https://www.youngminds.org.uk/parent/a-z-guide/school-anxiety-and-refusal/
- https://childmind.org/article/back-school-anxiety/

Chapter 24: The teenage brain and mood difficulties

- **Self-help guides**
    - https://www.kidshealth.org.nz/adolescent-brain-development
    - https://raisingchildren.net.au/pre-teens/development/understanding-your-pre-teen/brain-development-teens

- https://www.claytonschools.net/cms/lib/MO01000419/Centricity/Domain/177/23.%20Beyond%20Raging%20Hormones.pdf
- https://www.nimh.nih.gov/health/publications/the-teen-brain-7-things-to-know
- https://www.youngminds.org.uk/media/xl2nf0df/young-minds-depression.pdf
- https://childmind.org/awareness-campaigns/childrens-mental-health-report/2017-childrens-mental-health-report/
- https://www.healthychildren.org/English/ages-stages/teen/Pages/Whats-Going-On-in-the-Teenage-Brain.aspx
- https://www.justonenorfolk.nhs.uk/childhood-development-additional-needs/supporting-development/teenage-brain

■ **Books**
- Siegel DJ & Bryson TP (2012) *The Whole-Brain Child.* New York, NY: Random House.
- Morgan N (2007) *Blame my Brain: The Amazing Teenage Brain Revealed.* London: Walker.
- Morgan N (2014) *The Teenage Guide to Stress.* London: Walker.
- Morgan N (2018) *The Teenage Guide to Life Online.* London: Walker Books Ltd.
- Morgan N & Cassidy C (2017) *The Teenage Guide to Friends.* London: Walker Books and Subsidiaries.
- Morgan N (2018) *Positively Teenage: A Positively Brilliant Guide to Teenage Well-Being.* London: Franklin Watts.
- Morgan N (2019) *Body brilliant: A Teenage Guide to a Positive Body Image.* London: Franklin Watts.
- Morgan N (2021) *The Awesome Power of Sleep: How Sleep Super-charges your Teenage Brain.* London: Walker Books Ltd.
- Morgan N (2021) *Be Resilient: How to Build a Strong Teenage Mind for Tough Times.* Newtown, N.S.W.: Walker Books.
- Morgan N (2020) *Exam attack: A practical, positive guide to exam success and beating stress.* London: Hachette Children's Group.
- Walsh D & Walsh E (2014) *Why Do They Act That Way? -Revised and Updated: A Survival Guide to the Adolescent Brain for You and Your Teen.* Simon and Schuster.
- Corbin B (2007) *Unleashing the potential of the teenage brain: Ten powerful ideas.* Corwin Press.

Chapter 25: Depression and low mood AND
Chapter 26: Specific strategies for depression

- **Self-help guides**
    - https://www.youngminds.org.uk/young-person/your-guide-to-support/guide-to-camhs/#WhatisCAMHS
    - https://www.youngminds.org.uk/parent/a-z-guide/depression-and-low-mood/
    - https://childmind.org/article/how-to-help-your-depressed-teenager
    - https://www.helpguide.org/articles/depression/parents-guide-to-teen-depression.htm
    - https://www.helpguide.org/articles/depression/teenagers-guide-to-depression.htm
    - https://www.nhsinform.scot/illnesses-and-conditions/mental-health/mental-health-self-help-guides/depression-self-help-guide
    - https://www.rcpsych.ac.uk/mental-health/parents-and-young-people/young-people/depression-in-children-and-young-people-for-young-people.
    - https://www.amh.org.uk/news/depression-in-young-people/
    - http://www.selfhelpguides.ntw.nhs.uk/iaptsheffield/leaflets/selfhelp/Depression%20and%20Low%20Mood.pdf
    - https://www.cbtregisteruk.com/

- **Books**
    - **For parents:**
        - Erika's Lighthouse (2019) *Parent Handbook on Childhood and Teen Depression*. Pennsauken: BookBaby.
    - **For children:**
        - Huebner D & Matthews B (2007) *What to do when you grumble too much: A kid's guide to overcoming negativity.* Washington, D.C: Magination Press.
    - **For young people / teens:**
        - Collins-Donnelly K & Gothard T (2018) *Starving the Depression Gremlin: A Cognitive Behavioural Therapy Workbook on Managing Depression for Young People.* London: Jessica Kingsley Publishers.

- Hurley K & Blackwell A (2019) *The Depression Workbook for Teens: Tools to Improve Your Mood, Build Self-Esteem, and Stay Motivated.* San Antonio: Althea Press.
- Schab L (2012) *Beyond the Blues: A Workbook to Help Teens Overcome Depression.* Oakland: Instant Help.

- **Mental health apps**
  - https://www.camhs-resources.co.uk/apps-1
- **Journals**
  - https://www.independent.co.uk/extras/indybest/kids/books/best-kids-journal-child-gratitude-happy-b1821016.html
  - Chapter 26: Specific strategies for depression
  - https://www.cci.health.wa.gov.au/-/media/CCI/Consumer-Modules/Back-from-The-Bluez/Back-from-the-Bluez---02---Behavioural-Strategies.pdf
  - https://www.cci.health.wa.gov.au/Resources/Looking-After-Yourself/Sleep
- **When to seek professional help**
  - https://www.nice.org.uk/guidance/ng134/chapter/Recommendations#step-3-managing-mild-depression
  - https://www.nice.org.uk/guidance/ng134
- **What to do in times of emergency**
  - NHS helplines:
    - https://www.nhs.uk/mental-health/nhs-voluntary-charity-services/charity-and-voluntary-services/get-help-from-mental-health-helplines/
    - England: https://www.nhs.uk/service-search/mental-health/find-an-urgent-mental-health-helpline
    - Scotland: https://clearyourhead.scot/support
    - Northern Ireland: https://www.lifelinehelpline.info/
    - Wales: https://sbuhb.nhs.wales/urgent-care-out-of-hours/mental-health-crisis/

- Papyrus: Mental health charity for young people. They offer confidential support and advice to young people struggling with thoughts of suicide, and anyone worried about a young person through their helpline, HopeLineUK: https://www.papyrus-uk.org/.
- Self-harm guide for parents and carers from the University of Oxford: https://www.psych.ox.ac.uk/news/new-guide-for-parents-who-are-coping-with-their-child2019s-self-harm-2018you-are-not-alone2019
- YoungMinds Textline support for mental health for young people: "If you feel unable to cope or need to get something off your chest, our trained volunteers will listen. We can support you with take steps towards helping you feeling better. Whatever you're going through, you are not alone." https://www.youngminds.org.uk/young-person/youngminds-textline/
- British Medical Journal Best Practice: https://bestpractice.bmj.com/topics/en-gb/785
- https://bestpractice.bmj.com/patient-leaflets/engb/html/1503893856127/Depression%20in%20children%20and%20teenagers%3A%20what%20is%20it%3F

- **Social media and depression**
    - https://www.huffingtonpost.co.uk/2016/02/12/social-media-affects-child-mental-health_n_9202460.html
    - https://www.internetmatters.org/hub/expert-opinion/social-media-impact-mental-health-young-people/?gclid = CjwKCAjwiY6MBhBqEiwARFSCPpmRxrP6TqGunKVrJL3Awvj3nzT4UcLMdrYnrlqY6PhXa8qfCBzk6BoC0ckQAvD_BwE
    - https://www.nationalbullyinghelpline.co.uk/cyberbullying.html#

References

Action Mental Health (2021) Depression in young people – recognising the signs and knowing where to get help. Available at: https://www.amh.org.uk/news/depression-in-young-people/

Adan, R., van der Beek, E.M., Buitelaar, J.K., Cryan, J.F., Hebebrand, J., Higgs, S., Schellekens, H. & Dickson, S.L. (2019) Nutritional psychiatry: Towards improving mental health by what you eat. *European neuropsychopharmacology: the journal of the European College of Neuropsychopharmacology* 29 (12), 1321–1332.

Response Ability: *Social and Emotional Wellbeing: A Teacher's Guide.* Available at: https://s3-ap-southeast-2.amazonaws.com/himh/assets/Uploads/responseability-teachers-guide.pdf

YoungMinds: *Parents survival guide.* Available at: www.youngminds.org.uk/parent/survival-guide/

YoungMinds: *Supporting your child with anxiety: A guide for parents.* Available at: https://youngminds.org.uk/find-help/for-parents/parents-guide-to-support-a-z/parents-guide-to-support-anxiety/#what-is-anxiety?

Ainsworth, M.D.S. & Bowlby, J. (1991) An ethological approach to personality development. *American Psychologist* 46 (4) 333-341.

Allen, J., Rapee, R. & Sandberg, S. (2012). Assessment of maternally reported life events in children and adolescents: A comparison of interview and checklist methods. *Journal of Psychopathology and Behavioral Assessment,* 34, 204-215.

American Psychiatric Association (2013b) *Diagnostic and Statistical Manual of Mental Disorders (DSM-5).* Arlington, VA: Author.

American Psychological Association (2021) *Anxiety.* Available at: https://www.apa.org/topics/anxiety

American Psychological Association (2021) *Depression.* Available at: https://www.apa.org/topics/anxiety

Anna Freud National Centre for Children and Families: *Self-care.* Available at: https://www.annafreud.org/on-my-mind/self-care/

Anna Freud National Centre for Children and Families: *Whole-school approach.* Available at: https://www.mentallyhealthyschools.org.uk/whole-school-approach

Anxiety Canada: *Self-Help: Managing Your Phobia.* Available at: https://www.anxietycanada.com/sites/default/files/adult_hmspecific.pdf

BABCP: The online CBT Register for the UK and Ireland: https://www.cbtregisteruk.com/

BACP (2021) *BACP Mindometer report 2021.* Available at: https://www.bacp.co.uk/media/12065/bacp-mindometer-report-2021.pdf

Barton, J. (2021) *15 best kids' journals to draw in and write down their feelings.* Available at: https://www.independent.co.uk/extras/indybest/kids/books/best-kids-journal-child-gratitude-happy-b1821016.html

Beck, A.T. (1967) *Depression: Causes and treatment.* University of Pennsylvania Press.

Beck, A.T. (1997) The past and future of cognitive therapy. *Journal of Psychotherapy Practice & Research* 6 (4), 276–284.

Beck, A.T., Rush, A.J., Shaw, B.F. & Emery, G. (1979) *Cognitive Therapy of Depression.* New York, NY: Guilford Press.

Bignardi, G., Dalmaijer, E.S., Anwyl-Irvine, A.L., Smith, T.A., Siugzdaite, R., Uh, S. & Astle, D.E. (2020) Longitudinal increases in childhood depression symptoms during the COVID-19 lockdown. *Archives of disease in childhood,* 106(8), 791–797.

Body Dysmorphic Disorder Foundation (2021) *What is Body Dysmorphic Disorder?* Available at: https://bddfoundation.org/information/what-is-bdd/

Boyles, O. (2018) *10 Foods that Boost Mental Health.* Available at: https://www.icanotes.com/2018/04/04/10-foods-that-boost-mental-health/

British Medical Journal Best Practice (2021) *Depression in children*. Available at: https://bestpractice.bmj.com/topics/en-gb/785

Burns, D. (1989) *The Feeling Good Handbook*. New York, NY: Harper-Collins Publishers.

CAMHS Resources: *Apps*. Available at: https://www.camhs-resources.co.uk/apps-1

Carter, T., Pascoe, M., Bastounis, A., Morres, I., Callaghan, P. & Parker, A. (2021) The effect of physical activity on anxiety in children and young people: a systematic review and meta-analysis. *Journal of Affective Disorders* 285 10-21.

Centre for Clinical Interventions (2021) *Sleep hygiene*. Available at: https://www.cci.health.wa.gov.au/Resources/Looking-After-Yourself/Sleep

Centre for Clinical Interventions: *Back from the Bluez: Behavioural Strategies for Managing Depression*. Available at: https://www.cci.health.wa.gov.au/-/media/CCI/Consumer-Modules/Back-from-The-Bluez/Back-from-the-Bluez---02---Behavioural-Strategies.pdf

Centre for Clinical Interventions: *Sleep*. Available at: https://www.cci.health.wa.gov.au/Resources/Looking-After-Yourself/Sleep

Centre for Mental Health (2020) *Covid-19 and the nation's mental health. Forecasting needs and risks in the UK*. Available at: https://www.centreformentalhealth.org.uk/sites/default/files/2020-05/CentreforMentalHealth_COVID_MH_Forecasting_May20.pdf

Child Mind Institute (2017). *2017 Children's Mental Health Report*. Available at: https://childmind.org/awareness-campaigns/childrens-mental-health-report/2017-childrens-mental-health-report/

Child Mind Institute (2020) *What to Do (and Not Do) When Children Are Anxious*. Available at: https://childmind.org/article/what-to-do-and-not-do-when-children-are-anxious/

Child Mind Institute: *What Is Separation Anxiety?* Available at: https://childmind.org/article/what-is-separation-anxiety/

Child Mind Institute: *What to Do if You Think Your Teenager Is Depressed*. Available at: https://childmind.org/article/how-to-help-your-depressed-teenager

Clinical Partners (2021) Treatment for Depression in Teenagers and Children. Available at: https://www.clinical-partners.co.uk/child-adolescents/a-z-of-issues/depression-in-children/treatment-for-depression-in-teenagers-and-children

Costello, E.J., Egger, H.L. & Angold, A. (2005) The developmental epidemiology of anxiety disorders: phenomenology, prevalence, and comorbidity. *Child and adolescent psychiatric clinics of North America*, 14 (4), 631–vii.

Crocq, M.A. (2015) A history of anxiety: from Hippocrates to DSM.

Department of Health & Department for Education (2017) *Transforming Children and Young People's Mental Health Provision: a Green Paper*. Available at: https://assets.publishing.service.gov.uk/government/uploads/system/uploads/attachment_data/file/664855/Transforming_children_and_young_people_s_mental_health_provision.pdf

Douglas, P., Douglas, D., Harrigan, D., Douglas, K. (2009) Preparing for pandemic influenza and its aftermath: Mental health issues considered. *International Journal of Emergency Mental Health* 11 137-44.

Dunning, D.L., Griffiths, K., Kuyken, W., Crane, C., Foulkes, L., Parker, J. & Dalgleish, T. (2019) Research Review: The effects of mindfulness-based interventions on cognition and mental health in children and adolescents - a meta-analysis of randomized controlled trials. *Journal of Child Psychology and Psychiatry, and allied disciplines* 60 (3) 244–258.

Ehlers, A. & Clark, D.M. (2000). A cognitive model of posttraumatic stress disorder. *Behaviour Research and Therapy* 38 (4), 319–345.

Geddes, H. (2006) *Attachment in the classroom: The links between children's early experience, emotional well-being, and performance in school*. Worth Publishing.

Geddes, H. (2018). *Attachment, Behaviour and Learning*. Therapy Route. Available at: https://www.therapyroute.com/article/attachment-behaviour-and-learning-by-h-geddes

Getselfhelp: *Unhelpful Thinking Habits*. Available at: http://www.getselfhelp.co.uk/unhelpful.htm

Gökçe, G. & Yilmaz, B. (2018). Emotional Availability of Parents and Psychological Health: What Does Mediate This Relationship? *Journal of Adult Development.* 25 37-47.

Goldstein, C. (2021) *What to Do (and Not Do) When Children Are Anxious.* Available at: https://childmind.org/article/what-to-do-and-not-do-when-children-are-anxious/

Goodall, B., Chadwick, I., McKinnon, A., Werner-Seidler, A., Meiser-Stedman, R., Smith, P. & Dalgleish, T. (2017), Translating the Cognitive Model of PTSD to the Treatment of Very Young Children: A Single Case Study of an 8-Year-Old Motor Vehicle Accident Survivor. *Journal of Clinical Psychology* 73 511-523.

Greenberger, D. & Padesky, C.A. (2016) *Mind over mood: Change how you feel by changing the way you think.* New York, NY: Guilford Press.

Harvard Health Publishing: *Understanding the stress response.* Available at: https://www.health.harvard.edu/staying-healthy/understanding-the-stress-response

Headteacher Update (2018) *Attachment Theory in Schools.* Available at: https://www.headteacher-update.com/best-practice-article/attachment-theory-in-schools/167068/

Healthy Children (2019) *What's Going on in the Teenage Brain?* Available at: https://www.healthychildren.org/English/ages-stages/teen/Pages/Whats-Going-On-in-the-Teenage-Brain.aspx

Heinze, K., Cumming, J., Dosanjh, A., Palin, S., Poulton, S., Bagshaw, A.P. & Broome, M.R. (2021) Neurobiological evidence of longer-term physical activity interventions on mental health outcomes and cognition in young people: A systematic review of randomised controlled trials. *Neuroscience and biobehavioral reviews* 120 431–441.

HelpGuide (2021) *Body Dysmorphic Disorder (BDD).* Available at: https://www.helpguide.org/articles/anxiety/body-dysmorphic-disorder-bdd.htm

HelpGuide: *Helping Children Cope with Traumatic Events.* Available at: https://www.helpguide.org/articles/ptsd-trauma/helping-children-cope-with-traumatic-stress.htm

HelpGuide: *Parent's Guide to Teen Depression:* Available at: https://www.helpguide.org/articles/depression/parents-guide-to-teen-depression.htm

Hofmann, S.G., Asnaani, A., Vonk, I.J., Sawyer, A.T. & Fang, A. (2012) The Efficacy of Cognitive Behavioral Therapy: A Review of Meta-analyses. *Cognitive therapy and research* 36 (5), 427–440.

https://assets.publishing.service.gov.uk/government/uploads/system/uploads/attachment_data/file/213765/dh_123985.pdf

https://dictionary.apa.org/agoraphobia

https://www.nhs.uk/mental-health/conditions/agoraphobia/overview/.

Huebner, D. & Matthews, B. (2009) *What to Do When You Worry Too Much: A Kid's Guide to Overcoming Anxiety.* Paw Prints.

Huebner, D. & McHale, K. (2020) *Something bad happened: A kid's guide to coping with difficult world news.* London: Jessica Kingsley Publishers.

Jantz, G.L. (2016) *The Power of Positive Self-Talk.* Available at: https://www.psychologytoday.com/us/blog/hope-relationships/201605/the-power-positive-self-talk

KidsHealth (2021) *Adolescent Brain Development.* Available at: https://www.kidshealth.org.nz/adolescent-brain-development

Kim, Y.K. (2019) Panic Disorder: Current Research and Management Approaches. *Psychiatry investigation* 16 (1), 1–3.

Knoff, W.F. (1970) A history of the concept of neurosis, with a memoir of William Cullen. *The American Journal of Psychiatry,* 127(1), 80–84.

March, J.S., & Benton, C.M. (2006). *Talking Back to OCD: The Program That Helps Kids and Teens Say "No Way" – and Parents Say "Way to Go".* New York, Guilford Press.

Maslow, A.H. (1943) A Theory of Human Motivation. *Psychological Review* 50 (4), 430-437.

Mead, E. (2021) *What is Positive Self-Talk?* Available at: https://positivepsychology.com/positive-self-talk/

Meltzer, L.J. & Crabtree, V.M. (2015) *Pediatric Sleep Problems: A Clinician's Guide to Behavioral Interventions.* Washington, DC: APA Books.

Mental Health Foundation (2017) *Food for thought: Mental health and nutrition briefing.* Available at: https://www.mentalhealth.org.uk/sites/default/files/food-for-thought-mental-health-nutrition-briefing-march-2017.pdf

Mental Health Foundation (2019) *Body image: How we think and feel about our bodies.* Available at: https://www.mentalhealth.org.uk/publications/body-image-report

Mental Health Foundation: *Mental health in schools: Make it Count.* Available at: https://www.mentalhealth.org.uk/campaigns/mental-health-schools-make-it-count-scotland

Mind: *Phobias.* Available at: https://www.mind.org.uk/information-support/types-of-mental-health-problems/phobias/types-of-phobia/

National Bullying Helpline: *Cyberbullying and online harassment advice.* Available at: https://www.nationalbullyinghelpline.co.uk/cyberbullying.html

National Institute for Health and Care Excellence (2011) *Common mental health problems: identification and pathways to care: Clinical guideline [CG123]* Available at: https://www.nice.org.uk/guidance/CG123/chapter/1-Guidance#steps-2-and-3-treatment-and-referral-for-treatment

National Institute of Mental Health (2020) *The Teen Brain: 7 Things to Know.* Available at: https://www.nimh.nih.gov/health/publications/the-teen-brain-7-things-to-know

New York Times (2016) *Outsmarting Our Primitive Responses to Fear.* Available at: https://www.nytimes.com/2017/10/26/well/live/fear-anxiety-therapy.html

NHS (2020) *Depression in children and young people.* Available at: https://www.nhs.uk/mental-health/children-and-young-adults/advice-for-parents/children-depressed-signs/

NHS (2020) *Helping Your Child with OCD – A Parent / Carer Self Help Guide.* Available at: https://www.anxietyuk.org.uk/wp-content/uploads/2020/10/Helping-your-child-with-Obsessive-Compulsive-Disorder.pdf

NHS (2020) *Signs of an anxiety disorder.* Available at: https://www.nhs.uk/mental-health/feelings-symptoms-behaviours/feelings-and-symptoms/anxiety-disorder-signs/

NHS Child and Adolescent Mental Health Services (2021) *Depression / Low mood.* Available at: https://camhs.elft.nhs.uk/Conditions/Depression--Low-mood

NHS Digital (2017) *Mental Health of Children and Young People in England, 2017.* Available at: https://digital.nhs.uk/data-and-information/publications/statistical/mental-health-of-children-and-young-people-in-england/2017/2017

NHS Digital (2020) *Mental Health of Children and Young People in England, 2020: Wave 1 follow up to the 2017 survey.* Available at: https://digital.nhs.uk/data-and-information/publications/statistical/mental-health-of-children-and-young-people-in-england/2020-wave-1-follow-up

NHS Inform (2021): *Phobias.* Available at: https://www.nhsinform.scot/illnesses-and-conditions/mental-health/phobias

NHS inform: *Anxiety disorders in children.* Available at: https://www.nhsinform.scot/illnesses-and-conditions/mental-health/anxiety-disorders-in-children/

NICE (2005) *Obsessive-compulsive disorder and body dysmorphic disorder: treatment.* Available at: https://www.nice.org.uk/guidance/cg31/informationforpublic

NICE (2016) *Mental health problems in people with learning disabilities: prevention, assessment and management.* Available at: https://www.nice.org.uk/guidance/ng54

Norfolk and Waveney Children & Young People's Health Services (2021) *Teenage Brain.* Available at: https://www.justonenorfolk.nhs.uk/childhood-development-additional-needs-supporting-development/teenage-brain

OCD UK (2021) *Excoriation Disorder (skin picking disorder).* Available at: https://www.ocduk.org/related-disorders/skin-picking/

OCD UK (2021) *Related Disorders.* Available at: https://www.ocduk.org/related-disorders/

OCD UK (2021) *Trichotillomania (Hair Pulling Disorder).* Available at: https://www.ocduk.org/related-disorders/trichotillomania/

Office for National Statistics (2020) *Children's views on well-being and what makes a happy life, UK.* Available at: https://www.ons.gov.uk/peoplepopulationandcommunity/wellbeing/articles/childrensviewsonwellbeingandwhatmakesahappylifeuk2020/2020-10-02

O'Reilly, M. (2020) Social media and adolescent mental health: the good, the bad and the ugly. *Journal of Mental Health* 29:2, 200-206.

Papadopoulos, L. (2017) *How does social media impact the mental health of young people?* Available at: https://www.internetmatters.org/hub/expert-opinion/social-media-impact-mental-health-young-people/

Perciavalle, V., Blandini, M., Fecarotta, P., Buscemi, A., Di Corrado, D., Bertolo, L., Fichera, F. & Coco, M.(2017) The role of deep breathing on stress. *Neurological Sciences* 38: 451-458.

Pereira, A.I., Barros, L., Mendonça, D. & Muris. P. (2013) The relationships among parental anxiety, parenting, and children's anxiety: The mediating effects of children's cognitive vulnerabilities. *Journal of Child and Family Studies* 23 (2) 399-409.

Plaisted, H., Waite, P., Gordon, K. & Creswell, C. (2021) Optimising Exposure for Children and Adolescents with Anxiety, OCD and PTSD: A Systematic Review. *Clinical child and family psychology review* 24 (2), 348–369.

Plummer, D., Harper, A. & ProQuest (Firm) (2010) *Helping children to cope with change, stress, and anxiety: A photocopiable activities book.* London: Jessica Kingsley Publishers.

Rachman, S. (2015) The evolution of behaviour therapy and cognitive behaviour therapy. *Behaviour Research and Therapy*, 64, 1-8.

Royal College of Psychiatrists (2021) *Cognitive Behavioural Therapy (CBT): for Parents and young people.* Available at: https://www.rcpsych.ac.uk/mental-health/parents-and-young-people/young-people/cognitive-behavioural-therapy-(cbt)-for-parents-and-young-people

Royal College of Psychiatrists (2021) *Depression in children and young people: for young people.* Available at: https://www.rcpsych.ac.uk/mental-health/parents-and-young-people/young-people/depression-in-children-and-young-people-for-young-people

Salkovskis, P.M., Forrester, E. & Richards, C. (1998) Cognitive–behavioural approach to understanding obsessional thinking. *The British Journal of Psychiatry*, 173(S35), 53-63.

Sarchiapone, M., Mandelli, L., Carli, V., Iosue, M., Wasserman, C., Hadlaczky, G., Hoven, C.W., Apter, A., Balazs, J., Bobes, J., Brunner, R., Corcoran, P., Cosman, D., Haring, C., Kaess, M., Keeley, H., Keresztény, A., Kahn, J.P., Postuvan, V., Mars, U., Saiz, P.A., Varnik, P., Sisask, M. & Wasserman, D. (2014) Hours of sleep in adolescents and its association with anxiety, emotional concerns, and suicidal ideation. *Sleep medicine* 15 (2) 248–254.

Schnackenberg, N. (2021) Young people's experiences of body dysmorphic disorder in education settings: a grounded theory. *Educational Psychology in Practice* 37:2, 202-220.

Siegel, D.J. & Bryson, T.P. (2012) *The Whole-Brain Child.* New York, NY: Random House.

Smith, P., Perrin, S., Yule, W. & Clark, D.M. (2010) *Post-Traumatic Stress Disorder: Cognitive Therapy with Children and Young People (1st ed.).* London: Routledge.

Sohn, S., Rees, P., Wildridge, B., Kalk, N. & Carter, B. (2019). Prevalence of problematic smartphone usage and associated mental health outcomes amongst children and young people: systematic review, meta-analysis, and GRADE of the evidence. *BMC Psychiatry* 19 356.

Stallard, P. (2009) *Anxiety: Cognitive Behaviour Therapy with Children and Young People.* London: Routledge.

Stallard, P. (2018) *Think Good, Feel Good: A Cognitive Behavioural Therapy Workbook for Children and Young People, 2nd Edition.* John Wiley and Sons

The TLC Foundation for Body-Focused Repetitive Behaviors (2021) *What is Excoriation (Skin Picking) Disorder?* Available at: https://www.bfrb.org/learn-about-bfrbs/skin-picking-disorder

Thing, C., Lim-Ashworth, N., Poh, B. & Lim, C.G. (2020). Recent developments in the intervention of specific phobia among adults: a rapid review. *F1000Research* 9 F1000 Faculty Rev-195.

Toussaint, L., Nguyen, Q.A., Roettger, C., Dixon, K., Offenbächer, M., Kohls, N., Hirsch, J. & Sirois, F. (2021). Effectiveness of Progressive Muscle Relaxation, Deep Breathing, and Guided Imagery in Promoting Psychological and Physiological States of Relaxation. *Evidence-Based Complementary and Alternative Medicine* 5924040.

Veale, D., Gledhill, L.J., Christodoulou, P. & Hodsoll, J. (2016) Body dysmorphic disorder in different settings: A systematic review and estimated weighted prevalence. *Body Image* 18 168–186.

Verduyn, C., Rogers, J. & Wood, A. (2009) Depression: Cognitive behaviour therapy with children and young people. Routledge.

Waite P, Pearcey S, Shum A, Raw J, Patalay P & Creswell C (2020) *How did the mental health of children and adolescents change during early lockdown during the COVID-19 pandemic in the UK?* Available at: https://doi.org/10.31234/osf.io/t8rfx

Waite, P., & Williams, T. (eds.) (2009) *Obsessive Compulsive Disorder: Cognitive Behaviour Therapy with Children and Young People*. London: Routledge.

Walkup, J.T., Albano, A.M., Piacentini, J., Birmaher, B., Compton, S.N., Sherrill, J.T., Ginsburg, G.S., Rynn, M.A., McCracken, J., Waslick, B., Iyengar, S., March, J.S. & Kendall, P.C. (2008) Cognitive behavioral therapy, sertraline, or a combination in childhood anxiety. *The New England journal of medicine*, 359 (26), 2753–2766.

Willetts, L. & Creswell, C. (2007) *Overcoming your child's shyness and social anxiety: a self-help guide using cognitive behavioral techniques*. London: Constable & Robinson.

World Health Organization (2021) Depression. Available at: https://www.who.int/health-topics/depression#tab = tab_1

World Health Organization (2021) *ICD-11: International Classification of Diseases 11th Revision.* Available at: https://www.who.int/standards/classifications/classification-of-diseases

www.justonenorfolk.nhs.uk

YMCA (2016) *It's time to Be Real about body image*. Available at: https://www.ymca.co.uk/health-and-wellbeing/feature/its-time-be-real-about-body-image

YoungMinds (2021) *Coronavirus: Impact on young people with mental health needs*. Available at: https://www.youngminds.org.uk/media/esifqn3z/youngminds-coronavirus-report-jan-2021.pdf

YoungMinds *Depression: Your guide to depression and finding the help and support you need.* Available at: https://www.youngminds.org.uk/media/xl2nf0df/young-minds-depression.pdf

YoungMinds: *School anxiety and refusal: A guide for parents*. Available at: https://www.youngminds.org.uk/parent/parents-a-z-mental-health-guide/school-anxiety-and-refusal/

YoungMinds: *Supporting your child with anxiety: A guide for parents*. Available at: https://youngminds.org.uk/find-help/for-parents/parents-guide-to-support-a-z/parents-guide-to-support-anxiety/

How to Help

To keep up to date with the *How to Help* series, bookmark:
www.pavpub.com/howtohelp